PENGUIN BOOKS — GREAT IDEAS

Eichmann and the Holocaust

Hannah Arendt
1906–1975

Hannah Arendt

Eichmann and the Holocaust

PENGUIN BOOKS — GREAT IDEAS

PENGUIN BOOKS

Published by the Penguin Group
Penguin Group (USA) Inc., 375 Hudson Street, New York, New York 10014, U.S.A.
Penguin Group (Canada), 90 Eglinton Avenue East, Suite 700, Toronto,
Ontario, Canada M4P 2Y3 (a division of Pearson Penguin Canada Inc.)
Penguin Books Ltd, 80 Strand, London WC2R 0RL, England
Penguin Ireland, 25 St Stephen's Green, Dublin 2, Ireland (a division of Penguin Books Ltd)
Penguin Group (Australia), 250 Camberwell Road, Camberwell,
Victoria 3124, Australia (a division of Pearson Australia Group Pty Ltd)
Penguin Books India Pvt Ltd, 11 Community Centre, Panchsheel Park, New Delhi – 110 017, India
Penguin Group (NZ), cnr Airborne and Rosedale Roads, Albany,
Auckland 1310, New Zealand (a division of Pearson New Zealand Ltd)
Penguin Books (South Africa) (Pty) Ltd, 24 Sturdee Avenue,
Rosebank, Johannesburg 2196, South Africa

Penguin Books Ltd, Registered Offices:
80 Strand, London WC2R 0RL, England

This edition published in Penguin Books (UK) 2005
Published in Penguin Books (USA) 2006

1   3   5   7   9   10   8   6   4   2

Reprinted from *Eichmann in Jerusalem*
(The Viking Press, 1963; Penguin Books, 1977).

ISBN 0 14 30.3760 9
CIP data available

Printed in the United States of America
Set in Monotype Dante

The following selections are excerpted from Eichmann in
Jerusalem: A Report on the Banality of Evil *and based on*
'A Reporter at Large: Eichmann in Jerusalem', *a five-part article
Arendt was commissioned to write for* The New Yorker.
*The parts appeared on 16 February 1963, 23 February 1963,
2 March 1963, 9 March 1963, and 16 March 1963.
The presiding judge of the trial was Moshe Landau. The chief
prosecutor was the attorney general, Gideon Hausner. Adolf
Eichmann was represented by Dr Robert Servatius.*

An Expert on the Jewish Question

IN 1934, when Eichmann applied successfully for a job,
the SD* was a relatively new apparatus in the SS,
founded two years earlier by Heinrich Himmler to serve
as the Intelligence service of the Party and now headed by
Reinhardt Heydrich, a former Navy Intelligence officer,
who was to become, as Gerald Reitlinger put it, 'the real
engineer of the Final Solution' (*The Final Solution*, 1961).
Its initial task had been to spy on Party members, and
thus to give the SS an ascendancy over the regular Party
apparatus. Meanwhile it had taken on some additional

---

* SD = *Sicherheitsdienst* (the Security Service of the SS).

duties, becoming the information and research centre for the Secret State Police, or Gestapo. These were the first steps toward the merger of the SS and the police, which, however, was not carried out until September 1939, although Himmler held the double post of Reichsführer SS and Chief of the German Police from 1936 on. Eichmann, of course, could not have known of these future developments, but he seems to have known nothing either of the nature of the SD when he entered it; this is quite possible, because the operations of the SD had always been top secret. As far as he was concerned, it was all a misunderstanding and at first 'a great disappointment. For I thought this was what I had read about in the *Münchener Illustrierten Zeitung*; when the high Party officials drove along, there were commando guards with them, men standing on the running boards of the cars ... In short, I had mistaken the Security Service of the Reichsführer SS for the Reich Security Service ... and nobody set me right and no one told me anything. For I had had not the slightest notion of what now was revealed to me.' The question of whether he was telling the truth had a certain bearing on the trial, where it had to be decided whether he had volunteered for his position or had been drafted into it. His misunderstanding, if such it was, is not inexplicable; the SS or *Schutzstaffeln* had originally been established as special units for the protection of the Party leaders.

His disappointment, however, consisted chiefly in that he had to start all over again, that he was back at the bottom, and his only consolation was that there were others who had made the same mistake. He was put into the Information department, where his first job was to file all information concerning Freemasonry (which in the early Nazi ideological muddle was somehow lumped with Judaism, Catholicism, and Communism) and to help in the establishment of a Freemasonry museum. He now had ample opportunity to learn what this strange word meant that Kaltenbrunner had thrown at him in their discussion of Schlaraffia. (Incidentally, an eagerness to establish museums commemorating their enemies was very characteristic of the Nazis. During the war, several services competed bitterly for the honour of establishing anti-Jewish museums and libraries. We owe to this strange craze the salvage of many great cultural treasures of European Jewry.) The trouble was that things were again very, very boring, and he was greatly relieved when, after four or five months of Freemasonry, he was put into the brand-new department concerned with Jews. This was the real beginning of the career which was to end in the Jerusalem court.

It was the year 1935, when Germany, contrary to the stipulations of the Treaty of Versailles, introduced general conscription and publicly announced plans for rearmament, including the building of an air force and a navy. It was also the year when Germany, having left the League of Nations in 1933, prepared neither quietly nor secretly the occupation of the demilitarized zone of the Rhineland. It was the time of Hitler's peace speeches – 'Germany needs peace and desires peace,' 'We recognize Poland as the home of a great and nationally conscious people,' 'Germany neither intends nor wishes to interfere in the internal affairs of Austria, to annex

Austria, or to conclude an *Anschluss'* – and, above all, it was the year when the Nazi regime won general and, unhappily, genuine recognition in Germany and abroad, when Hitler was admired everywhere as a great national statesman. In Germany itself, it was a time of transition. Because of the enormous rearmament programme, unemployment had been liquidated, the initial resistance of the working class was broken, and the hostility of the regime, which had at first been directed primarily against 'anti-Fascists' – Communists, Socialists, left-wing intellectuals, and Jews in prominent positions – had not yet shifted entirely to persecution of the Jews qua Jews.

To be sure, one of the first steps taken by the Nazi government, back in 1933, had been the exclusion of Jews from the Civil Service (which in Germany included all teaching positions, from grammar school to university, and most branches of the entertainment industry, including radio, the theatre, the opera, and concerts) and, in general, their removal from public office. But private business remained almost untouched until 1938, and even the legal and medical professions were only gradually abolished, although Jewish students were excluded from most universities and were nowhere permitted to graduate. Emigration of Jews in these years proceeded in a not unduly accelerated and generally orderly fashion, and the currency restrictions that made it difficult, but not impossible, for Jews to take their money, or at least the greater part of it, out of the country were the same for non-Jews; they dated back to the days of the Weimar Republic. There were a certain number of *Einzelaktionen*, individual actions putting pressure on Jews to sell their

4

property at often ridiculously low prices, but these usually occurred in small towns and, indeed, could be traced to the spontaneous, 'individual' initiative of some enterprising Storm Troopers, the so-called SA men, who, except for their officer corps, were mostly recruited from the lower classes. The police, it is true, never stopped these 'excesses', but the Nazi authorities were not too happy abut them, because they affected the value of real estate all over the country. The emigrants, unless they were political refugees, were young people who realized that there was no future for them in Germany. And since they soon found out that there was hardly any future for them in other European countries either, some Jewish emigrants actually returned during this period. When Eichmann was asked how he had reconciled his personal feelings about Jews with the outspoken and violent anti-Semitism of the Party he had joined, he replied with the proverb: 'Nothing's as hot when you eat it as when it's being cooked' – a proverb that was then on the lips of many Jews as well. They lived in a fool's paradise, in which, for a few years, even Streicher spoke of a 'legal solution' of the Jewish problem. It took the organized pogroms of November 1938, the so-called *Kristallnacht* or Night of Broken Glass, when seventy-five hundred Jewish shop windows were broken, all synagogues went up in flames, and twenty thousand Jewish men were taken off to concentration camps, to expel them from it.

The frequently forgotten point of the matter is that the famous Nuremberg Laws, issued in the fall of 1935, had failed to do the trick. The testimony of three witnesses from Germany, high-ranking former officials of the Zionist organization who left Germany shortly before the outbreak of the war, gave only the barest glimpse into the true state of affairs during the first five years of the Nazi regime. The Nuremberg Laws had deprived the Jews of their political but not of their civil rights; they were no longer citizens (*Reichsbürger*), but they remained members of the German state (*Staatsangehörige*). Even if they emigrated, they were not automatically stateless. Sexual intercourse between Jews and Germans, and the contraction of mixed marriages, were forbidden. Also, no German woman under the age of forty-five could be employed in a Jewish household. Of these stipulations, only the last was of practical significance; the others merely legalized a *de facto* situation. Hence, the Nuremberg Laws were felt to have stabilized the new situation of Jews in the German Reich. They had been second-class citizens, to put it mildly, since January 30, 1933; their almost complete separation from the rest of the population had been achieved in a matter of weeks or months – through terror but also through the more than ordinary connivance of those around them. 'There was a wall between Gentiles and Jews,' Dr Benno Cohn of Berlin testified. 'I cannot remember speaking to a Christian during all my journeys over Germany.' Now, the Jews felt, they had received laws of their own and would no longer be outlawed. If they kept to themselves, as they had been forced to do anyhow, they would be able to live unmolested. In the words of the *Reichsvertretung* of the Jews in Germany (the national association of all communities and organizations, which had been founded in September 1933 on the initiative of the Berlin community, and was in no way Nazi-appointed), the intention of the Nuremberg Laws was 'to establish a level on which a bearable relationship between the German and the Jewish people [became] possible', to which a member of the Berlin community, a radical Zionist, added: 'Life is possible under every law. However, in complete ignorance of what is permitted and what is not one cannot live. A useful and respected citizen one can also be as a member of a minority in the midst of a great people' (Hans Lamm, *Über die Entwicklung des deutschen Judentums*, 1951). And since Hitler, in the Röhm purge in 1934, had broken the power of the SA, the Storm Troopers in brown shirts who had been almost exclusively responsible for the early pogroms and atrocities, and since the Jews were blissfully unaware of the growing power of the black-shirted SS, who ordinarily abstained from what Eichmann contemptuously called the '*Stürmer* methods', they generally believed that a *modus vivendi* would be possible; they even offered to cooperate in 'the solution of the Jewish question'. In short, when Eichmann entered upon his apprenticeship in Jewish affairs, on which, four years later, he was to be the recognized 'expert', and when he made his first contacts with Jewish functionaries, both Zionists and Assimilationists talked in terms of a great 'Jewish revival', a 'great constructive movement of German Jewry', and they still quarrelled among themselves in ideological terms about the desirability of Jewish emigration, as though this depended upon their own decisions.

Eichmann's account during the police examination of

how he was introduced into the new department – distorted, of course, but not wholly devoid of truth – oddly recalls this fool's paradise. The first thing that happened was that his new boss, a certain von Mildenstein, who shortly thereafter got himself transferred to Albert Speer's *Organisation Todt*, where he was in charge of highway construction (he was what Eichmann pretended to be, an engineer by profession), required him to read Theodor Herzl's *Der Judenstaat*, the famous Zionist classic, which converted Eichmann promptly and forever to Zionism. This seems to have been the first serious book he ever read and it made a lasting impression on him. From then on, as he repeated over and over, he thought of hardly anything but a 'political solution' (as opposed to the later 'physical solution', the first meaning expulsion and the second extermination) and how to 'get some firm ground under the feet of the Jews'. (It may be worth mentioning that, as late as 1939, he seems to have protested against desecrators of Herzl's grave in Vienna, and there are reports of his presence in civilian clothes at the commemoration of the thirty-fifth anniversary of Herzl's death. Strangely enough, he did not talk about these things in Jerusalem, where he continuously boasted of his good relations with Jewish officials.) In order to help in this enterprise, he began spreading the gospel among his SS comrades, giving lectures and writing pamphlets. He then acquired a smattering of Hebrew, which enabled him to read haltingly a Yiddish newspaper – not a very difficult accomplishment, since Yiddish, basically an old German dialect written in Hebrew letters, can be understood by any German-speaking person who has mastered a few dozen Hebrew words. He even read one more book, Adolf Böhm's *History of Zionism* (during the trial he kept confusing it with Herzl's *Judenstaat*), and this was perhaps a considerable achievement for a man who, by his own account, had always been utterly reluctant to read anything except newspapers, and who, to the distress of his father, had never availed himself of the books in the family library. Following up Böhm, he studied the organizational setup of the Zionist movement, with all its parties, youth groups, and different programmes. This did not yet make him an 'authority', but it was enough to earn him an assignment as official spy on the Zionist offices and on their meetings; it is worth noting that his schooling in Jewish affairs was almost entirely concerned with Zionism.

His first personal contacts with Jewish functionaries, all of them well-known Zionists of long standing, were thoroughly satisfactory. The reason he became so fascinated by the 'Jewish question', he explained, was his own 'idealism'; these Jews, unlike the Assimilationists, whom he always despised, and unlike Orthodox Jews, who bored him, were 'idealists', like him. An 'idealist', according to Eichmann's notions, was not merely a man who believed in an 'idea' or someone who did not steal or accept bribes, though these qualifications were indispensable. An 'idealist' was a man who *lived* for his idea – hence he could not be a businessman – and who was prepared to sacrifice for his idea everything and, especially, everybody. When he said in the police examination that he would have sent his own father to his death if that had been required, he did not mean merely to stress the extent to which he was under orders, and ready to obey them; he also meant to show what an 'idealist' he had always been. The perfect 'idealist', like everybody else, had of course his personal feelings and emotions, but he would never permit them to interfere with his actions if they came into conflict with his 'idea'. The greatest 'idealist' Eichmann ever encountered among the Jews was Dr Rudolf Kastner, with whom he negotiated during the Jewish deportations from Hungary and with whom he came to an agreement that he, Eichmann, would permit the 'illegal' departure of a few thousand Jews to Palestine (the trains were in fact guarded by German police) in exchange for 'quiet and order' in the camps from which hundreds of thousands were shipped to Auschwitz. The few thousand saved by the agreement, prominent Jews and members of the Zionist youth organizations, were, in Eichmann's words, 'the best biological material'. Dr Kastner, as Eichmann understood it, had sacrificed his fellow-Jews to his 'idea', and this was as it should be. Judge Benjamin Halevi, one of the three judges at Eichmann's trial, had been in charge of the Kastner trial in Israel, at which Kastner had to defend himself for his cooperation with Eichmann and other high-ranking Nazis; in Halevi's opinion, Kastner had 'sold his soul to the devil'. Now that the devil himself was in the dock he turned out to be an 'idealist', and though it may be hard to believe, it is quite possible that the one who sold his soul had also been an 'idealist'.

Long before all this happened, Eichmann was given

his first opportunity to apply in practice what he had learned during his apprenticeship. After the *Anschluss* (the incorporation of Austria into the Reich), in March 1938, he was sent to Vienna to organize a kind of emigration that had been utterly unknown in Germany, where up to the fall of 1938 the fiction was maintained that Jews if they so desired were permitted, but were not forced, to leave the country. Among the reasons German Jews believed in the fiction was the programme of the NSDAP, formulated in 1920, which shared with the Weimar Constitution the curious fate of never being officially abolished; its Twenty-Five Points had even been declared 'unalterable' by Hitler. Seen in the light of later events, its anti-Semite provisions were harmless indeed: Jews could not be full-fledged citizens, they could not hold Civil Service positions, they were to be excluded from the press, and all those who had acquired German citizenship after 2 August 1914 – the date of the outbreak of the First World War – were to be denaturalized, which meant they were subject to expulsion. (Characteristically, the denaturalization was carried out immediately, but the wholesale expulsion of some fifteen thousand Jews, who from one day to the next were shoved across the Polish border at Zbaszyn, where they were promptly put into camps, took place only five years later, when no one expected it any longer.) The Party programme was never taken seriously by Nazi officials; they prided themselves on belonging to a movement, as distinguished from a party, and a movement could not be bound by a programme. Even before the Nazis' rise to power, these Twenty-Five Points had been no more than a concession to the party system and to such prospective voters as were old-fashioned enough to ask what was the programme of the party they were going to join. Eichmann, as we have seen, was free of such deplorable habits, and when he told the Jerusalem court that he had not known Hitler's programme he very likely spoke the truth: 'The Party programme did not matter, you knew what you were joining.' The Jews, on the other hand, were old-fashioned enough to know the Twenty-Five Points by heart and to believe in them; whatever contradicted the legal implementation of the Party programme they tended to ascribe to temporary, 'revolutionary excesses' of undisciplined members or groups.

But what happened in Vienna in March 1938 was altogether different. Eichmann's task had been defined as 'forced emigration', and the words meant exactly what they said: all Jews, regardless of their desires and regardless of their citizenship, were to be forced to emigrate – an act which in ordinary language is called expulsion. Whenever Eichmann thought back to the twelve years that were his life, he singled out his year in Vienna as head of the Centre for Emigration of Austrian Jews as its happiest and most successful period. Shortly before, he had been promoted to officer's rank, becoming an *Untersturmführer*, or lieutenant, and he had been commended for his 'comprehensive knowledge of the methods of organization and ideology of the opponent, Jewry'. The assignment in Vienna was his first important job; his whole career, which had progressed rather slowly, was in the balance. He must have been frantic to make good, and his success was spectacular: in eight

months, forty-five thousand Jews left Austria, whereas
no more than nineteen thousand left Germany in the
same period; in less than eighteen months, Austria was
'cleansed' of close to a hundred and fifty thousand
people, roughly sixty per cent of its Jewish population,
all of whom left the country 'legally', even after the
outbreak of the war, some sixty thousand Jews could
escape. How did he do it? The basic idea that made all
this possible was of course not his but, almost certainly,
a specific directive by Heydrich, who had sent him to
Vienna in the first place. (Eichmann was vague on the
question of authorship, which he claimed, however, by
implication; the Israeli authorities, on the other hand,
bound (as Yad Vashem's *Bulletin* put it) to the fantastic 'thesis of the all-inclusive responsibility of Adolf
Eichmann' and the even more fantastic 'supposition
that one [i.e., his] mind was behind it all', helped him
considerably in his efforts to deck himself in borrowed
plumes, for which he had in any case a great inclination.)
The idea, as explained by Heydrich in a conference with
Göring on the morning of the *Kristallnacht*, was simple
and ingenious enough: 'Through the Jewish community,
we extracted a certain amount of money from the rich
Jews who wanted to emigrate. By paying this amount,
and an additional sum in foreign currency, they made it
possible for poor Jews to leave. The problem was not to
make the rich Jews leave, but to get rid of the Jewish
mob.' And this 'problem' was not solved by Eichmann.
Not until the trial was over was it learned from the
Netherlands State Institute for War Documentation that
Erich Rajakowitsch, a 'brilliant lawyer' whom Eichmann,

according to his own testimony, 'employed for the handling of legal questions in the central offices for Jewish emigration in Vienna, Prague, and Berlin', had originated the idea of the 'emigration funds'. Somewhat later, in April 1941, Rajakowitsch was sent to Holland by Heydrich in order to 'establish there a central office which was to serve as a model for the "solution of the Jewish question" in all occupied countries in Europe'.

Still, enough problems remained that could be solved only in the course of the operation, and there is no doubt that here Eichmann, for the first time in his life, discovered in himself some special qualities. There were two things he could do well, better than others: he could organize and he could negotiate. Immediately upon his arrival, he opened negotiations with the representatives of the Jewish community, whom he had first to liberate from prisons and concentration camps, since the 'revolutionary zeal' in Austria, greatly exceeding the early 'excesses' in Germany, had resulted in the imprisonment of practically all prominent Jews. After this experience, the Jewish functionaries did not need Eichmann to convince them of the desirability of emigration. Rather, they informed him of the enormous difficulties which lay ahead. Apart from the financial problem, already 'solved', the chief difficulty lay in the number of papers every emigrant had to assemble before he could leave the country. Each of the papers was valid only for a limited time, so that the validity of the first had usually expired long before the last could be obtained. Once Eichmann understood how the whole thing worked, or, rather, did not work, he 'took counsel with himself' and 'gave birth to the idea which I thought would do justice to both parties'. He imagined 'an assembly line, at whose beginnings the first document is put, and then the other papers, and at its end the passport would have to come out as the end product'. This could be realized if all the officers concerned – the Ministry of Finance, the income tax people, the police, the Jewish community, etc. – were housed under the same roof and forced to do their work on the spot, in the presence of the applicant, who would no longer have to run from office to office and who, presumably, would also be spared having some humiliating chicaneries practiced on him, and certain expenses for bribes. When everything was ready and the assembly line was doing its work smoothly and quickly, Eichmann 'invited' the Jewish functionaries from Berlin to inspect it. They were appalled: 'This is like an automatic factory, like a flour mill connected with some bakery. At one end you put in a Jew who still has some property, a factory, or a shop, or a bank account, and he goes through the building from counter to counter, from office to office, and comes out at the other end without any money, without any rights, with only a passport on which it says: "You must leave the country within a fortnight. Otherwise you will go to a concentration camp."'

This, of course, was essentially the truth about the procedure, but it was not the whole truth. For these Jews could not be left 'without any money', for the simple reason that without it no country at this date would have taken them. They needed, and were given, their *Vorzeigegeld*, the amount they had to show in order to obtain their visas and to pass the immigration controls of the recipient country. For this amount, they needed foreign currency, which the Reich had no intention of wasting on its Jews. These needs could not be met by Jewish accounts in foreign countries, which, in any event, were difficult to get at because they had been illegal for many years; Eichmann therefore sent Jewish functionaries abroad to solicit funds from the great Jewish organizations, and these funds were then sold by the Jewish community to the prospective emigrants at a considerable profit – one dollar, for instance, was sold for 10 or 20 marks when its market value was 4.20 marks. It was chiefly in this way that the community acquired not only the money necessary for poor Jews and people without accounts abroad, but also the funds it needed for its own hugely expanded activities. Eichmann did not make possible this deal without encountering considerable opposition from the German financial authorities, the Ministry and the Treasury, which, after all, could not remain unaware of the fact that these transactions amounted to a devaluation of the mark.

Bragging was the vice that was Eichmann's undoing. It was sheer rodomontade when he told his men during the last days of the war: 'I will jump into my grave laughing, because the fact that I have the death of five million Jews [or 'enemies of the Reich', as he always claimed to have said] on my conscience gives me extraordinary satisfaction.' He did not jump, and if he had anything on his conscience, it was not murder but, as it turned out, that he had once slapped the face of Dr Josef Löwenherz, head of the Vienna Jewish community, who later became one of his favourite Jews. (He had apologized in front of his staff at the time, but this incident kept bothering him.) To claim the death of five million Jews, the approximate total of losses suffered from the combined efforts of all Nazi offices and authorities, was preposterous, as he knew very well, but he had kept repeating the damning sentence *ad nauseam* to everyone who would listen, even twelve years later in Argentina, because it gave him 'an extraordinary sense of elation to think that [he] was exiting from the stage in this way'. (Former Legationsrat Horst Grell, a witness for the defence, who had known Eichmann in Hungary, testified that in his opinion Eichmann was boasting. That must have been obvious to everyone who heard him utter his absurd claim.) It was sheer boasting when he pretended he had 'invented' the ghetto system or had 'given birth to the idea' of shipping all European Jews to Madagascar. The Theresienstadt ghetto, of which Eichmann claimed 'paternity', was established years after the ghetto system had been introduced into the Eastern occupied territories, and setting up a special ghetto for certain privileged categories was, like the ghetto system, the 'idea' of Heydrich. The Madagascar plan seems to have been 'born' in the bureaus of the German Foreign Office, and Eichmann's own contribution to it turned out to owe a good deal to his beloved Dr Löwenherz, whom he had drafted to put down 'some basic thoughts' on how about four million Jews might be transported from Europe after the war – presumably to Palestine, since the Madagascar project was top secret. (When confronted at the trial with the Löwenherz report, Eichmann did not deny its authorship; it was one of the few moments when he appeared genuinely embarrassed.) What eventually led to his capture was his compulsion to talk big – he was 'fed up with being an anonymous wanderer between the worlds' – and this compulsion must have grown considerably stronger as time passed, not only because he had nothing to do that he could consider worth doing, but also because the postwar era had bestowed so much unexpected 'fame' upon him.

But bragging is a common vice, and a more specific, and also more decisive, flaw in Eichmann's character was his almost total inability ever to look at anything from the other fellow's point of view. Nowhere was this flaw more conspicuous than in his account of the Vienna episode. He and his men and the Jews were all 'pulling together', and whenever there were any difficulties the Jewish functionaries would come running to him 'to unburden their hearts', to tell him 'all their grief and sorrow', and to ask for his help. The Jews 'desired' to emigrate, and he, Eichmann, was there to help them, because it so happened that at the same time the Nazi authorities had expressed a desire to see their Reich *judenrein*. The two desires coincided, and he, Eichmann, could 'do justice to both parties'. At the trial, he never gave an inch when it came to this part of the story, although he agreed that today, when 'times have changed so much', the Jews might not be too happy to recall this 'pulling together' and he did not want 'to hurt their feelings'.

The German text of the taped police examination, conducted from 29 May 1960 to 17 January 1961, each page corrected and approved by Eichmann, constitutes a veritable gold mine for a psychologist – provided he is wise enough to understand that the horrible can be not only ludicrous but outright funny. Some of the comedy cannot be conveyed in English, because it lies in Eichmann's heroic fight with the German language, which invariably defeats him. It is funny when he speaks, *passim*, of 'winged words' (*geflügelte Worte*, a German colloquialism for famous quotes from the classics) when he means stock phrases, *Redensarten*, or slogans, *Schlag-worte*. It was funny when, during the cross-examination on the Sassen documents, conducted in German by the presiding judge, he used the phrase '*kontra geben*' (to give tit for tat), to indicate that he had resisted Sassen's efforts to liven up his stories; Judge Landau, obviously ignorant of the mysteries of card games, did not understand, and Eichmann could not think of any other way to put it. Dimly aware of a defect that must have plagued him even in school – it amounted to a mild case of aphasia – he apologized, saying, 'Officialese [*Amtssprache*] is my only language.' But the point here is that officialese became his language because he was genuinely incapable of uttering a single sentence that was not a cliché. (Was it these clichés that the psychiatrists thought so 'normal' and 'desirable'? Are these the 'positive ideas' a clergy-man hopes for in those to whose souls he ministers? Eichmann's best opportunity to show this positive side of his character in Jerusalem came when the young police officer in charge of his mental and psychological well-being handed him *Lolita* for relaxation. After two days Eichmann returned it, visibly indignant; 'Quite an unwholesome book' – '*Das ist aber ein sehr unerfreuliches*

Buch' – he told his guard.) To be sure, the judges were right when they finally told the accused that all he had said was 'empty talk' – except that they thought the emptiness was feigned, and that the accused wished to cover up other thoughts which, though hideous, were not empty. This supposition seems refuted by the striking consistency with which Eichmann, despite his rather bad memory, repeated word for word the same stock phrases and self-invented clichés (when he did succeed in constructing a sentence of his own, he repeated it until it became a cliché) each time he referred to an incident or event of importance to him. Whether writing his memoirs in Argentina or in Jerusalem, whether speaking to the police examiner or to the court, what he said was always the same, expressed in the same words. The longer one listened to him, the more obvious it became that his inability to speak was closely connected with an inability to *think*, namely, to think from the standpoint of somebody else. No communication was possible with him, not because he lied but because he was surrounded by the most reliable of all safeguards against the words and the presence of others, and hence against reality as such.

Thus, confronted for eight months with the reality of being examined by a Jewish policeman, Eichmann did not have the slightest hesitation in explaining to him at considerable length, and repeatedly, why he had been unable to attain a higher grade in the SS, and that this was not his fault. He had done everything, even asked to be sent to active military duty – 'Off to the front, I said to myself, then the *Standartenführer* [colonelcy] will come quicker.' In court, on the contrary, he pretended he had asked to be transferred because he wanted to escape his murderous duties. He did not insist much on this, though, and, strangely, he was not confronted with his utterances to Captain Less, whom he also told that he had hoped to be nominated for the *Einsatzgruppen*, the mobile killing units in the East, because when they were formed, in March 1941, his office was 'dead' – there was no emigration any longer and deportations had not yet been started. There was, finally, his greatest ambition – to be promoted to the job of police chief in some German town; again, nothing doing. What makes these pages of the examination so funny is that all this was told in the tone of someone who was sure of finding 'normal, human' sympathy for a hard-luck story. 'Whatever I prepared and planned, everything went wrong, my personal affairs as well as my years-long efforts to obtain land and soil for the Jews. I don't know, everything was as if under an evil spell; whatever I desired and wanted and planned to do, fate prevented it somehow. I was frustrated in everything, no matter what.' When Captain Less asked his opinion on some damning and possibly lying evidence given by a former colonel of the SS, he exclaimed, suddenly stuttering with rage: 'I am very much surprised that this man could ever have been an SS *Standartenführer*, that surprises me very much indeed. It is altogether, altogether unthinkable. I don't know what to say.' He never said these things in a spirit of defiance, as though he wanted, even now, to defend the standards by which he had lived in the past. The very words 'SS', or 'career', or 'Himmler' (whom he always called by his long official title: Reichsführer SS and Chief of the German Police, although he by no means admired him) triggered in him a mechanism that had become completely unalterable. The presence of Captain Less, a Jew from Germany and unlikely in any case to think that members of the SS advanced in their careers through the exercise of high moral qualities, did not for a moment throw this mechanism out of gear.

Now and then, the comedy breaks into the horror itself, and results in stories, presumably true enough, whose macabre humour easily surpasses that of any Surrealist invention. Such was the story told by Eichmann during the police examination about the unlucky Kommerzialrat Storfer of Vienna, one of the representatives of the Jewish community. Eichmann had received a telegram from Rudolf Höss, Commandant of Auschwitz, telling him that Storfer had arrived and had urgently requested to see Eichmann. 'I said to myself: OK, this man has always behaved well, that is worth my while . . . I'll go there myself and see what is the matter with him. And I go to Ebner [chief of the Gestapo in Vienna], and Ebner says – I remember it only vaguely – "If only he had not been so clumsy; he went into hiding and tried to escape," something of the sort. And the police arrested him and sent him to the concentration camp, and, according to the orders of the Reichsführer [Himmler], no one could get out once he was in. Nothing could be done, neither Dr Ebner nor I nor anybody else could do anything about it. I went to Auschwitz and asked Höss to see Storfer. "Yes, yes [Höss said], he is in one of the labour gangs." With Storfer afterward, well, it was normal and human, we had a normal, human encounter. He told me all his grief and sorrow. I said: "Well, my dear old friend [*Ja, mein lieber guter Storfer*], we certainly got it! What rotten luck!" And I also said: "Look, I really cannot help you, because according to orders from the Reichsführer nobody can get out. I can't get you out. Dr Ebner can't get you out. I hear you made a mistake, that you went into hiding or wanted to bolt, which, after all, *you* did not need to do." [Eichmann meant that Storfer, as a Jewish functionary, had immunity from deportation.] I forget what his reply to this was. And then I asked him how he was. And he said, yes, he wondered if he couldn't be let off work, it was heavy work. And then I said to Höss: "Work – Storfer won't have to work!" But Höss said: "Everyone works here." So I said: "OK," I said, "I'll make out a chit to the effect that Storfer has to keep the gravel paths in order with a broom," there were little gravel paths there, "and that he has the right to sit down with his broom on one of the benches." [To Storfer] I said: "Will that be all right, Mr Storfer? Will that suit you?" Whereupon he was very pleased, and we shook hands, and then he was given the broom and sat down on his bench. It was a great inner joy to me that I could at least see the man with whom I had worked for so many long years, and that we could speak with each other.' Six weeks after this normal human encounter, Storfer was dead – not gassed, apparently, but shot.

Is this a textbook case of bad faith, of lying self-deception combined with outrageous stupidity? Or is it simply the case of the eternally unrepentant criminal (Dostoevsky once mentions in his diaries that in Siberia, among scores of murderers, rapists, and burglars, he never met a single man who would admit that he had done wrong) who cannot afford to face reality because his crime has become part and parcel of it? Yet Eichmann's case is different from that of the ordinary criminal, who can shield himself effectively against the reality of a non-criminal world only within the narrow limits of his gang. Eichmann needed only to recall the past in order to feel assured that he was not lying and that he was not deceiving himself, for he and the world he lived in had once been in perfect harmony. And that German society of eighty million people had been shielded against reality and factuality by exactly the same means, the same self-deception, lies, and stupidity that had now become ingrained in Eichmann's mentality. These lies changed from year to year, and they frequently contradicted each other; moreover, they were not necessarily the same for the various branches of the Party hierarchy or the people at large. But the practice of self-deception had become so common, almost a moral prerequisite for survival, that even now, eighteen years after the collapse of the Nazi regime, when most of the specific content of its lies has been forgotten, it is sometimes difficult not to believe that mendacity has become an integral part of the German national character. During the war, the lie most effective with the whole of the German people was the slogan of 'the battle of destiny for the German people' [*der Schicksalskampf des deutschen Volkes*], coined either by Hitler or by Goebbels, which made self-deception easier on three counts: it suggested, first, that the war was no war; second, that it was started by destiny and not by Germany; and, third, that it was a matter of life and death for the Germans, who must annihilate their enemies or be annihilated.

Eichmann's astounding willingness, in Argentina as well as in Jerusalem, to admit his crimes was due less to his own criminal capacity for self-deception than to the aura of systematic mendacity that had constituted the general, and generally accepted, atmosphere of the Third Reich. 'Of course' he had played a role in the extermination of the Jews; of course if he 'had not transported them, they would not have been delivered to the butcher'. 'What,' he asked, 'is there to "admit"?' Now, he proceeded, he 'would like to find peace with [his] former enemies' – a sentiment he shared not only with Himmler, who had expressed it during the last year of the war, or with the Labour Front leader Robert Ley (who, before he committed suicide in Nuremberg, had proposed the establishment of a 'conciliation committee' consisting of the Nazis responsible for the massacres and the Jewish survivors) but also, unbelievably, with many ordinary Germans, who were heard to express themselves in exactly the same terms at the end of the war. This outrageous cliché was no longer issued to them from above, it was a self-fabricated stock phrase, as devoid of reality as those clichés by which the people had lived for twelve years; and you could almost see what an 'extraordinary sense of elation' it gave to the speaker the moment it popped out of his mouth.

Eichmann's mind was filled to the brim with such

sentences. His memory proved to be quite unreliable about what had actually happened; in a rare moment of exasperation, Judge Landau asked the accused: 'What *can* you remember?' (if you don't remember the discussions at the so-called Wannsee Conference, which dealt with the various methods of killing) and the answer, of course, was that Eichmann remembered the turning points in his own career rather well, but that they did not necessarily coincide with the turning points in the story of Jewish extermination or, as a matter of fact, with the turning points in history. (He always had trouble remembering the exact date of the outbreak of the war or of the invasion of Russia.) But the point of the matter is that he had not forgotten a single one of the sentences of his that at one time or another had served to give him a 'sense of elation'. Hence, whenever, during the cross-examination, the judges tried to appeal to his conscience, they were met with 'elation', and they were outraged as well as disconcerted when they learned that the accused had at his disposal a different elating cliché for each period of his life and each of his activities. In his mind, there was no contradiction between 'I will jump into my grave laughing,' appropriate for the end of the war, and 'I shall gladly hang myself in public as a warning example for all anti-Semites on this earth,' which now, under vastly different circumstances, fulfilled exactly the same function of giving him a lift.

These habits of Eichmann's created considerable difficulty during the trial – less for Eichmann himself than for those who had come to prosecute him, to defend him, to judge him, and to report on him. For all this, it was essential that one take him seriously, and this was very hard to do, unless one sought the easiest way out of the dilemma between the unspeakable horror of the deeds and the undeniable ludicrousness of the man who perpetrated them, and declared him a clever, calculating liar – which he obviously was not. His own convictions in this matter were far from modest: 'One of the few gifts fate bestowed upon me is a capacity for truth insofar as it depends upon myself.' This gift he had claimed even before the prosecutor wanted to settle on him crimes he had not committed. In the disorganized, rambling notes he made in Argentina in preparation for the interview with Sassen, when he was still, as he even pointed out at the time, 'in full possession of my physical and psychological freedom', he had issued a fantastic warning to 'future historians to be objective enough not to stray from the path of this truth recorded here' – fantastic because every line of these scribblings shows his utter ignorance of everything that was not directly, technically and bureaucratically, connected with his job, and also shows an extraordinarily faulty memory.

Despite all the efforts of the prosecution, everybody could see that this man was not a 'monster', but it was difficult indeed not to suspect that he was a clown. And since this suspicion would have been fatal to the whole enterprise, and was also rather hard to sustain in view of the sufferings he and his like had caused to millions of people, his worst clowneries were hardly noticed and almost never reported. What could you do with a man who first declared, with great emphasis, that the one thing he had learned in an ill-spent life was that one should never take an oath ('Today no man, no judge could ever persuade me to make a sworn statement, to declare something under oath as a witness. I refuse it, I refuse it for moral reasons. Since my experience tells me that if one is loyal to his oath, one day he has to take the consequences, I have made up my mind once and for all that no judge in the world or any other authority will ever be capable of making me swear an oath, to give sworn testimony. I won't do it voluntarily and no one will be able to force me'), and then, after being told explicitly that if he wished to testify in his own defence he might 'do so under oath or without an oath,' declared without further ado that he would prefer to testify under oath? Or who, repeatedly and with a great show of feeling, assured the court, as he had assured the police examiner, that the worst thing he could do would be to try to escape his true responsibilities, to fight for his neck, to plead for mercy – and then, upon instruction of his counsel, submitted a handwritten document, containing his plea for mercy?

As far as Eichmann was concerned, these were questions of changing moods, and as long as he was capable of finding, either in his memory or on the spur of the moment, an elating stock phrase to go with them, he was quite content, without ever becoming aware of anything like 'inconsistencies'. As we shall see, this horrible gift for consoling himself with clichés did not leave him in the hour of his death.

The Final Solution: Killing

[. . .] In September 1941, shortly after his first official visits to the killing centres in the East, Eichmann organized his first mass deportations from Germany and the Protectorate, in accordance with a 'wish' of Hitler, who had told Himmler to make the Reich *judenrein* as quickly as possible. The first shipment contained twenty thousand Jews from the Rhineland and five thousand Gypsies, and in connection with this first transport a strange thing happened. Eichmann, who never made a decision on his own, who was extremely careful always to be 'covered' by orders, who – as freely given testimony from practically all the people who had worked with him confirmed – did not even like to volunteer suggestions and always required 'directives', now, 'for the first and last time', took an initiative contrary to orders: instead of sending these people to Russian territory, Riga or Minsk, where they would have immediately been shot by the *Einsatzgruppen*, he directed the transport to the ghetto of Lódz, where he knew that no preparations for extermination had yet been made – if only because the man in charge of the ghetto, a certain Regierungspräsident Uebelhör, had found ways and means of deriving considerable profit from 'his' Jews. (Lódz, in fact, was the first ghetto to be established and the last to be liquidated; those of its inmates who did not succumb to disease or starvation survived until the summer of 1944.) This decision was to get Eichmann into considerable trouble. The ghetto was overcrowded, and Mr Uebelhör was in no mood to receive newcomers and in no position to accommodate them. He was angry enough to complain to Himmler that Eichmann had deceived him and his men with 'horsetrading tricks learned from the Gypsies'. Himmler, as well as Heydrich, protected Eichmann and the incident was soon forgiven and forgotten.

Forgotten, first of all, by Eichmann himself, who did not once mention it either in the police examination or in his various memoirs. When he had taken the stand and was being examined by his lawyer, who showed him the documents, he insisted he had a 'choice': 'Here for the first and last time I had a choice . . . One was Lódz . . . If there are difficulties in Lódz, these people must be sent onward to the East. And since I had seen the preparations, I was determined to do all I could to send these people to Lódz by any means at my disposal.' Counsel for the defence tried to conclude from this incident that Eichmann had saved Jews whenever he could – which was patently untrue. The prosecutor, who cross-examined him later with respect to the same incident, wished to establish that Eichmann himself had determined the final destination of all shipments and hence had decided whether or not a particular trans-port was to be exterminated – which was also untrue. Eichmann's own explanation, that he had not disobeyed an order but only taken advantage of a 'choice', finally, was not true either, for there had been difficulties in Lódz, as he knew full well, so that his order read, in so many words: Final destination, Minsk or Riga. Although Eichmann had forgotten all about it, this was clearly the only instance in which he actually had tried to save Jews.

Three weeks later, however, there was a meeting in Prague, called by Heydrich, during which Eichmann stated that 'the camps used for the detention of [Russian] Communists [a category to be liquidated on the spot by the *Einsatzgruppen*] can also include Jews' and that he had 'reached an agreement' to this effect with the local commanders; there was also some discussion about the trouble at Lódz, and it was finally resolved to send fifty thousand Jews from the Reich (that is, including Austria, and Bohemia and Moravia) to the centres of the *Einsatzgruppen* operations at Riga and Minsk. Thus, we are perhaps in a position to answer Judge Landau's question – the question uppermost in the minds of nearly everyone who followed the trial – of whether the accused had a conscience: yes, he had a conscience, and his conscience functioned in the expected way for about four weeks, whereupon it began to function the other way around.

Even during those weeks when his conscience functioned normally, it did its work within rather odd limits. We must remember that weeks and months before he was informed of the Führer's order, Eichmann knew of the murderous activities of the *Einsatzgruppen* in the East; he knew that right behind the front lines all Russian functionaries ('Communists'), all Polish members of the professional classes, and all native Jews were being killed in mass shootings. Moreover, in July of the same year; a few weeks before he was called to Heydrich, he had received a memorandum from an SS man stationed in the Warthegau, telling him that 'Jews in the coming winter could no longer be fed,' and submitting for his consideration a proposal as to 'whether it would not be the most humane solution to kill those Jews who were incapable of work through some quicker means. This, at any rate, would be more agreeable than to let them die of starvation.' In an accompanying letter, addressed to 'Dear Comrade Eichmann', the writer admitted that 'these things sound sometimes fantastic, but they are quite feasible.' The admission shows that the much more 'fantastic' order of the Führer was not yet known to the writer, but the letter also shows to what extent this order was in the air. Eichmann never mentioned this letter and probably had not been in the least shocked by it. For this proposal concerned only *native* Jews, not Jews from the Reich or any of the Western countries. His conscience rebelled not at the idea of murder but at the idea of German Jews being murdered. ('I never denied that I knew that the *Einsatzgruppen* had orders to kill, but I did not know that Jews from the Reich evacuated to the East were subject to the same treatment. That is what I did not know.') It was the same with the conscience of a certain Wilhelm Kube, an old Party member and *Generalkommissar* in Occupied Russia, who was outraged when German Jews with the Iron Cross arrived in Minsk for 'special treatment'. Since Kube was more articulate than Eichmann, his words may give us an idea of what went on in Eichmann's head during the time he was plagued by his conscience: 'I am certainly tough and I am ready to help solve the Jewish question,' Kube wrote to his superior in December, 1941, 'but people who come from our own cultural milieu are certainly something else than the native animalized hordes.' This sort of conscience, which, if it rebelled at all, rebelled at murder of people 'from our own cultural milieu' has survived the Hitler regime; among Germans today, there exists a stubborn 'misinformation' to the effect that 'only' *Ostjuden*, Eastern European Jews, were massacred.

Nor is this way of thinking that distinguishes between the murder of 'primitive' and of 'cultured' people a monopoly of the German people. Harry Mulisch relates how, in connection with the testimony given by Professor Salo W. Baron about the cultural and spiritual achievements of the Jewish people, the following questions suddenly occurred to him: 'Would the death of the Jews have been less of an evil if they were a people without a culture, such as the Gypsies who were also exterminated? Is Eichmann on trial as a destroyer of human beings or as an annihilator of culture? Is a murderer of human beings more guilty when a culture is also destroyed in the process?' And when he put these questions to the Attorney General, it turned out – 'He [Hausner] thinks yes, I think no.' How ill we can afford to dismiss this matter, bury the troublesome question along with the past, came to light in the recent film *Dr Strangelove*, where the strange lover of the bomb – characterized, it is true, as a Nazi type – proposes to select in the coming disaster some hundred thousand persons to survive in underground shelters. And who are to be the happy survivors? Those with the highest IQ!

This question of conscience, so troublesome in Jerusalem, had by no means been ignored by the Nazi regime. On the contrary, in view of the fact that the participants in the anti-Hitler conspiracy of July 1944 very rarely mentioned the wholesale massacres in the East in their correspondence or in the statements they prepared for use in the event that the attempt on Hitler's life was successful, one is tempted to conclude that the Nazis greatly overestimated the practical importance of the problem. We may here disregard the early stages of the German opposition to Hitler, when it was still anti-Fascist and entirely a movement of the Left, which as a matter of principle accorded no significance to moral issues and even less to the persecution of the Jews – a mere 'diversion' from the class struggle that in the opinion of the Left determined the whole political scene. Moreover, this opposition had all but disappeared during the period in question – destroyed by the horrible terror of the SA troops in the concentration camps and Gestapo cellars, unsettled by full employment made possible through rearmament, demoralized by the Communist Party's tactic of joining the ranks of Hitler's party in order to install itself there as a 'Trojan horse'. What was left of this opposition at the beginning of the war – some trade-union leaders, some intellectuals of the 'homeless Left' who did not and could not know if there was anything behind them – gained its importance solely through the conspiracy which finally led to the 20th of July. (It is of course quite inadmissible to measure the strength of the German resistance by the number of those who passed through the concentration camps. Before the outbreak of the war, the inmates belonged in a great number of categories, many of which had nothing whatsoever to do with resistance of any kind: there were the wholly 'innocent' ones, such as the Jews; the 'asocials', such as confirmed criminals and homosexuals; Nazis who had been found guilty of something or other; etc. During the war the camps were populated by resistance fighters from all over occupied Europe.)

Most of the July conspirators were actually former Nazis or had held high office in the Third Reich. What had sparked their opposition had been not the Jewish question but the fact that Hitler was preparing war, and the endless conflicts and crises of conscience under which they laboured hinged almost exclusively on the problem of high treason and the violation of their loyalty oath to Hitler. Moreover, they found themselves on the horns of a dilemma which was indeed insoluble: in the days of Hitler's successes they felt they could do nothing because the people would not understand, and in the years of German defeats they feared nothing more than another 'stab-in-the-back' legend. To the last, their greatest concern was how it would be possible to prevent chaos and to ward off the danger of civil war. And the solution was that the Allies must be 'reasonable' and grant a 'moratorium' until order was restored – and with it, of course, the German Army's ability to offer resistance. They possessed the most precise knowledge of what was going on in the East, but there is hardly any doubt that not one of them would have dared even to think that the best thing that could have happened to Germany under the circumstances would have been open rebellion and civil war. The active resistance in Germany came chiefly from the Right, but in view of the past record of the German Social Democrats, it may be doubted that the situation would have been very different if the Left had played a larger part among the conspirators. The question is academic in any case, for no 'organized socialist resistance' existed in Germany during the war years – as the German historian, Gerhard Ritter, has rightly pointed out.

In actual fact, the situation was just as simple as it was hopeless: the overwhelming majority of the German people believed in Hitler – even after the attack on Russia and the feared war on two fronts, even after the United States entered the war, indeed even after Stalingrad, the defection of Italy, and the landings in France. Against this solid majority, there stood an indeterminate number of isolated individuals who were completely aware of the national and of the moral catastrophe; they might occasionally know and trust one another, there were friendships among them and an exchange of opinions, but no plan or intention of revolt. Finally there was the group of those who later became known as the conspirators, but they had never been able to come to an agreement on anything, not even on the question of conspiracy. Their leader was Carl Friedrich Goerdeler, former mayor of Leipzig, who had served three years under the Nazis as price-controller but had resigned rather early – in 1936. He advocated the establishment of a constitutional monarchy, and Wilhelm Leuschner, a representative of the Left, a former trade-union leader and Socialist, assured him of 'mass support'; in the Kreisau circle, under the influence of Helmuth von Moltke, there were occasional complaints raised that the rule of law was 'now trampled under foot', but the chief concern of this circle was the reconciliation of the two Christian churches and their 'sacred mission in the secular state', combined with an outspoken stand in favour of federalism. (On the political bankruptcy of the resistance movement as a whole since 1933 there is a well-documented, impartial study, the doctoral dissertation of George K. Romoser, soon to be published.)

As the war went on and defeat became more certain, political differences should have mattered less and political action become more urgent, but Gerhard Ritter seems right here too: 'Without the determination of [Count Klaus von] Stauffenberg, the resistance movement would have bogged down in more or less helpless inactivity.' What united these men was that they saw in Hitler a 'swindler', a 'dilettante', who 'sacrificed whole armies against the counsel of his experts', a 'madman' and a 'demon', 'the incarnation of all evil', which in the German context meant something both more and less than when they called him a 'criminal and a fool', which they occasionally did. But to hold such opinions about Hitler at this late date 'in no way precluded membership in the SS or the Party, or the holding of a government post' [Fritz Hesse], hence it did not exclude from the circle of the conspirators quite a number of men who themselves were deeply implicated in the crimes of the regime – as for instance Count Helldorf, then Police Commissioner of Berlin, who would have become Chief of the German Police if the coup d'état had been successful (according to one of Goerdeler's lists of prospective ministers); or Arthur Nebe of the RSHA, former commander of one of the mobile killing units in the East! In the summer of 1943, when the Himmler-directed extermination programme had reached its climax, Goerdeler was considering Himmler and Goebbels as potential allies, 'since these two men have realized that they are lost with Hitler'. (Himmler indeed became a 'potential ally' – though Goebbels did not – and was fully informed of their plans; he acted against the conspirators only after their failure.) I am quoting from the draft of a letter by Goerdeler to Field Marshal von Kluge; but these strange alliances cannot be explained away by 'tactical considerations' necessary vis-à-vis the Army commanders, for it was, on the contrary, Kluge and Rommel who had given 'special orders that those two monsters [Himmler and Göring] should be liquidated' [Ritter] – quite apart from the fact that Goerdeler's biographer, Ritter, insists that the above-quoted letter 'represents the most passionate expression of his hatred against the Hitler regime'.

No doubt these men who opposed Hitler, however belatedly, paid with their lives and suffered a most terrible death; the courage of many of them was admirable, but it was not inspired by moral indignation or by what they knew other people had been made to suffer; they were motivated almost exclusively by their conviction of the coming defeat and ruin of Germany. This is not to deny that some of them, such as Count York von Wartenburg, may have been roused to political opposition initially by 'the revolting agitation against the Jews in November 1938' [Ritter]. But that was the month when the synagogues went up in flames and the whole population seemed in the grip of some fear: houses of God had been set on fire, and believers as well as the superstitious feared the vengeance of God. To be sure, the higher officer corps was disturbed when Hitler's so-called 'commissar order' was issued in May 1941 and they learned that in the coming campaign against Russia all Soviet functionaries and naturally all Jews were simply to be massacred. In these circles, there was of course some concern about the fact that, as Goerdeler said, 'in the occupied areas and against the Jews techniques of liquidating human beings and of religious persecution are practised . . . which will always rest as a heavy burden on our history.' But it seems never to have occurred to them that this signified something more, and more dreadful, than that 'it will make our position [negotiating a peace treaty with the Allies] enormously difficult', that it was a 'blot on Germany's good name' and was undermining the morale of the Army. 'What on earth have they made of the proud army of the Wars of Liberation [against Napoleon in 1814] and of Wilhelm I [in the Franco-Prussian War of 1870],' Goerdeler cried when he heard the report of an SS man who 'nonchalantly related that it "wasn't exactly pretty to spray with machinegun fire ditches crammed with thousands of Jews and then to throw earth on the bodies that were still twitching".' Nor did it occur to them that these atrocities might be somehow connected with the Allies' demand for unconditional surrender, which they felt free to criticize as both 'nationalistic' and 'unreasonable', inspired by blind hatred. In 1943, when the eventual defeat of Germany was almost a certainty, and indeed even later, they still believed that they had a right to negotiate with their enemies 'as equals' for a 'just peace', although they knew only too well what an unjust and totally unprovoked war Hitler had started. Even more startling are their criteria for a 'just peace'. Goerdeler stated them again and again in numerous memoranda: 'the re-establishment of the national borders of 1914 [which meant the annexation of Alsace-Lorraine], with the addition of Austria and the Sudetenland'; furthermore, a 'leading position for Germany on the Continent' and perhaps the regaining of South Tyrol!

We also know from statements they prepared how they intended to present their case to the people. There is for instance a draft proclamation to the Army by General Ludwig Beck, who was to become chief of state, in which he talks at length about the 'obstinacy', the 'incompetence and lack of moderation' of the Hitler regime, its 'arrogance and vanity'. But the crucial point, 'the most unscrupulous act' of the regime, was that the Nazis wanted to hold 'the leaders of the armed forces responsible' for the calamities of the coming defeat; to which Beck added that crimes had been committed 'which are a blot on the honour of the German nation and a defilement of the good reputation it had gained in the eyes of the world'. And what would be the next step after Hitler had been liquidated? The German Army would go on fighting 'until an honourable conclusion of the war has been assured' – which meant the annexation of Alsace-Lorraine, Austria, and the Sudetenland. There is indeed every reason to agree with the bitter judgement on these men by the German novelist Friedrich P. Reck-Malleczewen, who was killed in a concentration camp on the eve of the collapse and did not participate in the anti-Hitler conspiracy. In his almost totally unknown 'Diary of a Man in Despair', (*Tagebuch eines Verzweifelten*,

1947), Reck-Malleczewen wrote, after he had heard of the failure of the attempt on Hitler's life, which of course he regretted: 'A little late, gentlemen, you who made this archdestroyer of Germany and ran after him, as long as everything seemed to be going well; you who . . . without hesitation swore every oath demanded of you and reduced yourselves to the despicable flunkies of this criminal who is guilty of the murder of hundreds of thousands, burdened with the lamentations and the curse of the whole world; now you have betrayed him . . . Now, when the bankruptcy can no longer be concealed, they betray the house that went broke, in order to establish a political alibi for themselves – the same men who have betrayed everything that was in the way of their claim to power.'

There is no evidence, and no likelihood, that Eichmann ever came into personal contact with the men of 20 July, and we know that even in Argentina he still considered them all to have been traitors and scoundrels. Had he ever had the opportunity, though, to become acquainted with Goerdeler's 'original' ideas on the Jewish question, he might have discovered some points of agreement. To be sure, Goerdeler proposed 'to pay indemnity to German Jews for their losses and mistreatment' – this in 1942, at a time when it was not only a matter of *German* Jews, and when these were not just being mistreated and robbed but *gassed;* but in addition to such technicalities, he had something more constructive in mind, namely, a 'permanent solution' that would 'save [all European Jews] from their unseemly position as a more or less undesirable "guest nation" in Europe'. (In Eichmann's jargon, this was called giving them 'some firm ground under their feet'.) For this purpose, Goerdeler claimed an 'independent state in a colonial country' – Canada or South America – a sort of Madagascar, of which he certainly had heard. Still, he made some concessions; not all Jews would be expelled. Quite in line with the early stages of the Nazi regime and the privileged categories which were then current, he was prepared 'not to deny German citizenship to those Jews who could produce evidence of special military sacrifice for Germany or who belonged to families with long-established traditions'. Well, whatever Goerdeler's 'permanent solution of the Jewish question' might have meant, it was not exactly 'original' – as Professor Ritter, even in 1954 full of admiration for his hero, called it – and Goerdeler would have been able to find plenty of 'potential allies' for this part of his programme too within the ranks of the Party and even the SS.

In the letter to Field Marshal von Kluge, quoted above, Goerdeler once appealed to Kluge's 'voice of conscience'. But all he meant was that even a general must understand that 'to continue the war with no chance for victory was an obvious crime'. From the accumulated evidence one can only conclude that conscience as such had apparently got lost in Germany, and this to a point where people hardly remembered it and had ceased to realize that the surprising 'new set of German values' was not shared by the outside world. This, to be sure, is not the entire truth. For there were individuals in Germany who from the very beginning of the regime and without ever wavering were opposed to Hitler; no one knows how many there were of them – perhaps a hundred thousand, perhaps many more, perhaps many fewer – for their voices were never heard. They could be found everywhere, in all strata of society, among the simple people as well as among the educated, in all parties, perhaps even in the ranks of the NSDAP. Very few of them were known publicly, as were the aforementioned Reck-Malleczewen or the philosopher Karl Jaspers. Some of them were truly and deeply pious, like an artisan of whom I know, who preferred having his independent existence destroyed and becoming a simple worker in a factory to taking upon himself the 'little formality' of entering the Nazi Party. A few still took an oath seriously and preferred, for example, to renounce an academic career rather than swear by Hitler's name. A more numerous group were the workers especially in Berlin, and Socialist intellectuals who tried to aid the Jews they knew. There were, finally, the two peasant boys whose story is related in Günther Weisenborn's *Der lautlose Aufstand* (1953), who were drafted into the SS at the end of the war and refused to sign; they were sentenced to death, and on the day of their execution they wrote in their last letter to their families: 'We two would rather die than burden our conscience with such terrible things. We know what the SS must carry out.' The position of these people, who, practically speaking, did nothing, was altogether different from that of the conspirators. Their ability to tell right from wrong had remained intact, and they never suffered a 'crisis of conscience'. There may also have been such persons among the members of the resistance, but they were hardly more numerous in the ranks of the conspirators than among the people at large. They were neither heroes nor saints, and they remained completely silent. Only on one occasion, in a single desperate gesture, did this wholly isolated and mute element manifest itself publicly: this was when the Scholls, two students at Munich University, brother and sister, under the influence of their teacher Kurt Huber, distributed the famous leaflets in which Hitler was finally called what he was – a 'mass murderer'.

If, however, one examines the documents and prepared statements of the so-called 'other Germany' that would have succeeded Hitler had the 20 July conspiracy succeeded, one can only marvel at how great a gulf separated even them from the rest of the world. How else can one explain the illusions of Goerdeler in particular or the fact that Himmler, of all people, but also Ribbentrop, should have started dreaming, during the last months of the war, of a magnificent new role as negotiators with the Allies for a defeated Germany. And if Ribbentrop certainly was simply stupid, Himmler, whatever else he might have been, was no fool.

The member of the Nazi hierarchy most gifted at solving problems of conscience was Himmler. He coined slogans, like the famous watchword of the SS, taken from a Hitler speech before the SS in 1931, 'My Honour is my Loyalty' – catch phrases which Eichmann called 'winged words' and the judges 'empty talk' – and issued them, as Eichmann recalled, 'around the turn of the year', presumably along with a Christmas bonus. Eichmann remembered only one of them and kept repeating it.

'These are battles which future generations will not have to fight again,' alluding to the 'battles' against women, children, old people, and other 'useless mouths'. Other such phrases, taken from speeches Himmler made to the commanders of the *Einsatzgruppen* and the Higher SS and Police Leaders, were: 'To have stuck it out and, apart from exceptions caused by human weakness, to have remained decent, that is what has made us hard. This is a page of glory in our history which has never been written and is never to be written.' Or: 'The order to solve the Jewish question, this was the most frightening order an organization could ever receive.' Or: We realize that what we are expecting from you is 'superhuman', to be 'superhumanly inhuman'. All one can say is that their expectations were not disappointed. It is noteworthy, however, that Himmler hardly ever attempted to justify in ideological terms, and if he did; it was apparently quickly forgotten. What stuck in the minds of these men who had become murderers was simply the notion of being involved in something historic, grandiose, unique ('a great task that occurs once in two thousand years'), which must therefore be difficult to bear. This was important, because the murderers were not sadists or killers by nature; on the contrary, a systematic effort was made to weed out all those who derived physical pleasure from what they did. The troops of the *Einsatzgruppen* had been drafted from the Armed SS, a military unit with hardly more crimes in its record than any ordinary unit of the German Army, and their commanders had been chosen by Heydrich from the SS, élite with academic degrees. Hence the problem was how to overcome not so much their conscience as the animal pity by which all normal men are affected in the presence of physical suffering. The trick used by Himmler – who apparently was rather strongly afflicted with these instinctive reactions himself – was very simple and probably very effective; it consisted in turning these instincts around, as it were, in directing them toward the self. So that instead of saying: What horrible things I did to people!, the murderers would be able to say: What horrible things I had to watch in the pursuance of my duties, how heavily the task weighed upon my shoulders!

Eichmann's defective memory where Himmler's ingenious watchwords were concerned may be an indication that there existed other and more effective devices for solving the problem of conscience. Foremost among them was, as Hitler had rightly foreseen, the simple fact of war. Eichmann insisted time and again on the 'different personal attitude' toward death when 'dead people were seen everywhere', and when everyone looked forward to his own death with indifference: 'We did not care if we died today or only tomorrow, and there were times when we cursed the morning that found us still alive.' Especially effective in this atmosphere of violent death was the fact that the Final Solution, in its later stages, was not carried out by shooting, hence through violence, but in the gas factories, which, from beginning to end, were closely connected with the 'euthanasia programme' ordered by Hitler in the first weeks of the war and applied to the mentally sick in Germany up to the invasion of Russia. The extermination programme that was started in the autumn of 1941 ran, as it were, on two altogether different tracks. One track led to the gas factories, and the other to the *Einsatzgruppen*, whose operations in the rear of the Army, especially in Russia, were justified by the pretext of partisan warfare, and whose victims were by no means only Jews. In addition to real partisans, they dealt with Russian functionaries, Gypsies, the asocial, the insane, and Jews. Jews were included as 'potential enemies', and, unfortunately, it was months before the Russian Jews came to understand this, and then it was too late to scatter. (The older generation remembered the First World War, when the German Army had been greeted as liberators; neither the young nor the old had heard anything about 'how Jews were treated in Germany, or, for that matter, in Warsaw'; they were 'remarkably ill-informed', as the German Intelligence service reported from White Russia (Hilberg). More remarkable, occasionally even German Jews arrived in these regions who were under the illusion they had been sent here as 'pioneers' for the Third Reich.) These mobile killing units, of which there existed just four, each of battalion size, with a total of no more than three thousand men, needed and got the close cooperation of the Armed Forces; indeed, relations between them were usually 'excellent' and in some instances 'affectionate' (*herzlich*). The generals showed a 'surprisingly good attitude toward the Jews'; not only did they hand their Jews over to the *Einsatzgruppen*, they often lent their own men, ordinary soldiers, to assist in the massacres. The total number of their Jewish victims is estimated by Hilberg to have reached almost a million and a half, but this was not the result of the Führer's order for the physical extermination of the whole Jewish people. It was the result of an earlier order, which Hitler gave to Himmler in March, 1941, to prepare the SS and the police 'to carry out special duties in Russia'.

The Führer's order for the extermination of all, not only Russian and Polish, Jews, though issued later, can be traced much further back. It originated not in the RSHA or in any of Heydrich's or Himmler's other offices, but in the Führer's Chancellery, Hitler's personal office. It had nothing to do with the war and never used military necessities as a pretext. It is one of the great merits of Gerald Reitlinger's *The Final Solution* to have proved, with documentary evidence that leaves no doubt, that the extermination programme in the Eastern gas factories grew out of Hitler's euthanasia programme; and it is deplorable that the Eichmann trial, so concerned with 'historical truth', paid no attention to this factual connection. This would have thrown some light on the much debated question of whether Eichmann, of the RSHA, was involved in *Gasgeschichten*. It is unlikely that he was, though one of his men, Rolf Günther, might have become interested of his own accord. Globocnik, for instance, who set up the gassing installations in the Lublin area, and whom Eichmann visited, did not address himself to Himmler or any other police or SS authority when he needed more personnel; he wrote to Viktor Brack, of the Führer's Chancellery, who then passed the request on to Himmler.

The first gas chambers were constructed in 1939, to

implement a Hitler decree dated September 1 of that year, which said that 'incurably sick persons should be granted a mercy death'. (It was probably this 'medical' origin of gassing that inspired Dr Servatius's amazing conviction that killing by gas must be regarded as 'a medical matter'.) The idea itself was considerably older. As early as 1935, Hitler had told his Reich Medical Leader Gerhard Wagner that 'if war came, he would take up and carry out this question of euthanasia, because it was easier to do so in wartime'. The decree was immediately carried out in respect to the mentally sick, and between December 1939 and August 1941 about fifty thousand Germans were killed with carbon-monoxide gas in institutions where the death rooms were disguised exactly as they later were in Auschwitz – as shower rooms and bathrooms. The programme was a flop. It was impossible to keep the gassing a secret from the surrounding German population; there were protests on all sides from people who presumably had not yet attained the 'objective' insight into the nature of medicine and the task of a physician. The gassing in the East – or, to use the language of the Nazis, 'the humane way' of killing 'by granting people a mercy death' – began on almost the very day when the gassing in Germany was stopped. The men who had been employed in the euthanasia programme in Germany were now sent east to build the new installations for the extermination of whole peoples – and these men came either from Hitler's Chancellery or from the Reich Health Department and were only now put under the administrative authority of Himmler.

None of the various 'language rules', carefully contrived to deceive and to camouflage, had a more decisive effect on the mentality of the killers than this first war decree of Hitler, in which the word for 'murder' was replaced by the phrase 'to grant a mercy death'. Eichmann, asked by the police examiner if the directive to avoid 'unnecessary hardships' was not a bit ironic, in view of the fact that the destination of these people was certain death anyhow, did not even understand the question, so firmly was it still anchored in his mind that the unforgivable sin was not to kill people but to cause unnecessary pain. During the trial, he showed unmistakable signs of sincere outrage when witnesses told of cruelties and atrocities committed by SS men – though the court and much of the audience failed to see these signs, because his single-minded effort to keep his self-control had misled them into believing that he was 'unmovable' and indifferent – and it was not the accusation of having sent millions of people to their death that ever caused him real agitation but only the accusation (dismissed by the court) of one witness that he had once beaten a Jewish boy to death. To be sure, he had also sent people into the area of the *Einsatzgruppen*, who did not 'grant a mercy death' but killed by shooting, but he was probably relieved when, in the later stages of the operation, this became unnecessary because of the ever-growing capacity of the gas chambers. He must also have thought that the new method indicated a decisive improvement in the Nazi government's attitude toward the Jews, since at the beginning of the gassing programme it had been expressly stated that the benefits of euthanasia were to be reserved for true Germans. As the war progressed, with violent and horrible death raging all around – on the front in Russia, in the deserts of Africa, in Italy, on the beaches of France, in the ruins of the German cities – the gassing centres in Auschwitz and Chelmno, in Majdanek and Belzek, in Treblinka and Sobibor, must actually have appeared the 'Charitable Foundations for Institutional Care' that the experts in mercy death called them. Moreover, from January 1942 on, there were euthanasia teams operating in the East to 'help the wounded in ice and snow', and though this killing of wounded soldiers was also 'top secret', it was known to many, certainly to the executors of the Final Solution.

It has frequently been pointed out that the gassing of the mentally sick had to be stopped in Germany because of protests from the population and from a few courageous dignitaries of the churches, whereas no such protests were voiced when the programme switched to the gassing of Jews, though some of the killing centres were located on what was then German territory and were surrounded by German populations. The protests, however, occurred at the beginning of the war; quite apart from the effects of 'education in euthanasia', the attitude toward a 'painless death through gassing' very likely changed in the course of the war. This sort of thing is difficult to prove; there are no documents to support it, because of the secrecy of the whole enterprise, and none of the war criminals ever mentioned it, not even the defendants in the Doctors' Trial at Nuremberg, who were full of quotations from the international literature on the subject. Perhaps they had forgotten the climate of public opinion in which they killed, perhaps they never cared to know it, since they felt, wrongly, that their 'objective and scientific' attitude was far more advanced than the opinions held by ordinary people. However, a few truly priceless stories, to be found in the war diaries of trustworthy men who were fully aware of the fact that their own shocked reaction was no longer shared by their neighbours, have survived the moral debacle of a whole nation.

Reck-Malleczewen, whom I mentioned before, tells of a female 'leader' who came to Bavaria to give the peasants a pep talk in the summer of 1944. She seems not to have wasted much time on 'miracle weapons' and victory; she faced frankly the prospect of defeat, about which no good German needed to worry because *the Führer 'in his great goodness had prepared for the whole German people a mild death through gassing in case the war should have an unhappy end'*. And the writer adds: 'Oh, no, I'm not imagining things, this lovely lady is not a mirage, I saw her with my own eyes: a yellow-skinned female pushing forty, with insane eyes . . . And what happened? Did these Bavarian peasants at least put her into the local lake to cool off her enthusiastic readiness for death? They did nothing of the sort. They went home, shaking their heads.'

My next story is even more to the point, since it concerns someone who was not a 'leader', may not even have been a Party member. It happened in Königsberg, in East Prussia, an altogether different corner of Germany, in January 1945, a few days before the Russians destroyed the city, occupied its ruins, and annexed the whole province. The story is told by Count Hans von Lehnsdorff, in his *Ostpreussisches Tagebuch* (1961). He had remained in the city as a physician to take care of wounded soldiers who could not be evacuated; he was called to one of the huge centres for refugees from the countryside, which was already occupied by the Red Army. There he was accosted by a woman who showed him a varicose vein she had had for years but wanted to have treated now, because she had time. 'I try to explain that it is more important for her to get away from Königsberg and to leave the treatment for some later time. Where do you want to go? I ask her. She does not know, but she knows that they will all be brought into the Reich. And then she adds, surprisingly: *"The Russians will never get us. The Führer will never permit it. Much sooner he will gas us."* I look around furtively, but no one seems to find this statement out of the ordinary.' The story, one feels, like most true stories, is incomplete. There should have been one more voice, preferably a female one, which, sighing heavily, replied: And now all that good, expensive gas has been wasted on the Jews!

The Wannsee Conference, or Pontius Pilate

My report on Eichmann's conscience has thus far followed evidence which he himself had forgotten. In his own presentation of the matter, the turning point came not four weeks but four months later, in January 1942, during the Conference of the *Staatssekretäre* (Undersecretaries of State), as the Nazis used to call it, or the Wannsee

Conference, as it now is usually called, because Heydrich had invited the gentlemen to a house in that suburb of Berlin. As the formal name of the conference indicates; the meeting had become necessary because the Final Solution, if it was to be applied to the whole of Europe, clearly required more than tacit acceptance from the Reich's State apparatus; it needed the active cooperation of all Ministries and of the whole Civil Service. The Ministers themselves, nine years after Hitler's rise to power, were all Party members of long standing – those who in the initial stages of the regime had merely 'coordinated' themselves, smoothly enough, had been replaced. Yet most of them were not completely trusted, since few among them owed their careers entirely to the Nazis, as did Heydrich or Himmler; and those who did, like Joachim von Ribbentrop, head of the Foreign Office, a former champagne salesman, were likely to be nonentities. The problem was much more acute, however, with respect to the higher career men in the Civil Service, directly under the Ministers, for these men, the backbone of every government administration, were not easily replaceable, and Hitler had tolerated them, just as Adenauer was to tolerate them, unless they were compromised beyond salvation. Hence the undersecretaries and the legal and other experts in the various Ministries were frequently not even Party members, and Heydrich's apprehensions about whether he would be able to enlist the active help of these people in mass murder were quite comprehensible. As Eichmann put it, Heydrich 'expected the greatest difficulties'. Well, he could not have been more wrong.

The aim of the conference was to coordinate all efforts toward the implementation of the Final Solution. The discussion turned first on 'complicated legal questions', such as the treatment of half- and quarter-Jews – should they be killed or only sterilized? This was followed by a frank discussion of the 'various types of possible solutions to the problem', which meant the various methods of killing, and here, too, there was more than 'happy agreement on the part of the participants'; the Final Solution was greeted with 'extraordinary enthusiasm' by all present, and particularly by Dr Wilhelm Stuckart, Undersecretary in the Ministry of the Interior, who was known to be rather reticent and hesitant in the face of 'radical' Party measures, and was, according to Dr Hans Globke's testimony at Nuremberg, a staunch supporter of the Law. There were certain difficulties, however. Undersecretary Josef Bühler, second in command in the General Government in Poland, was dismayed at the prospect that Jews would be evacuated from the West to the East, because this meant more Jews in Poland, and he proposed that these evacuations be postponed and that 'the Final Solution be started in the General Government, where no problems of transport existed'. The gentlemen from the Foreign Office appeared with their own carefully elaborated memorandum, expressing 'the desires and ideas of the Foreign Office with respect to the total solution of the Jewish question in Europe', to which nobody paid much attention. The main point, as Eichmann rightly noted, was that the members of the various branches of the Civil Service did not merely express opinions but made concrete propositions. The meeting lasted no more than an hour or an hour and a half, after which drinks were served and everybody had lunch – 'a cosy little social gathering', designed to strengthen the necessary personal contacts. It was a very important occasion for Eichmann, who had never before mingled socially with so many 'high personages'; he was by far the lowest in rank and social position of those present. He had sent out the invitations and had prepared some statistical material (full of incredible errors) for Heydrich's introductory speech – eleven million Jews had to be killed, an undertaking of some magnitude – and later he was to prepare the minutes. In short, he acted as secretary of the meeting. This was why he was permitted, after the dignitaries had left, to sit down near the fireplace with his chief Müller and Heydrich, 'and that was the first time I saw Heydrich smoke and drink'. They did not 'talk shop, but enjoyed some rest after long hours of work', being greatly satisfied and, especially Heydrich, in very high spirits.

There was another reason that made the day of this conference unforgettable for Eichmann. Although he had been doing his best right along to help with the Final Solution, he had still harboured some doubts about 'such a bloody solution through violence', and these doubts had now been dispelled. 'Here now, during this conference, the most prominent people had spoken, the Popes of the Third Reich.' Now he could see with his own eyes and hear with his own ears that not only Hitler, not only Heydrich or the 'sphinx' Müller, not just the SS or the Party, but the élite of the good old Civil Service were vying and fighting with each other for the honour of taking the lead in these 'bloody' matters. 'At that moment, I sensed a kind of Pontius Pilate feeling, for I felt free of all guilt.' *Who was he to judge?* Who was he 'to have [his] own thoughts in this matter'? Well, he was neither the first nor the last to be ruined by modesty.

What followed, as Eichmann recalled it, went more or less smoothly and soon became routine. He quickly became an expert in 'forced evacuation', as he had been an expert in 'forced emigration'. In country after country, the Jews had to register, were forced to wear the yellow badge for easy identification, were assembled and deported, the various shipments being directed to one or another of the extermination centres in the East, depending on their relative capacity at the moment; when a trainload of Jews arrived at a centre, the strong among them were selected for work, often operating the extermination machinery, all others were immediately killed. There were hitches, but they were minor. The Foreign Office was in contact with the authorities in those foreign countries that were either occupied or allied with the Nazis, to put pressure on them to deport their Jews, or, as the case might be, to prevent them from evacuating them to the East helter-skelter, out of sequence, without proper regard for the absorptive capacity of the death centres. (This was how Eichmann remembered it; it was in fact not quite so simple.) The legal experts drew up the necessary legislation for making the victims stateless, which was important on two counts: it made it impossible for any country to inquire into their fate, and it enabled the state in which they were resident to confiscate their property. The Ministry of Finance and the Reichsbank prepared facilities to receive the huge loot from all over Europe, down to watches and gold teeth, all of which was sorted out in the Reichsbank and then sent to the Prussian State Mint. The Ministry of Transport provided the necessary railroad cars, usually freight cars, even in times of great scarcity of rolling stock, and they saw to it that the schedule of the deportation trains did not conflict with other timetables. The Jewish Councils of Elders were informed by Eichmann or his men of how many Jews were needed to fill each train, and they made out the list of deportees. The Jews registered, filled out innumerable forms, answered pages and pages of questionnaires regarding their property so that it could be seized the more easily; they then assembled at the collection points and boarded the trains. The few who tried to hide or to escape were rounded up by a special Jewish police force. As far as Eichmann could see, no one protested, no one refused to cooperate. *'Immerzu fahren hier die Leute zu ihrem eigenen Begräbnis'* (Day in day out the people here leave for their own funeral), as a Jewish observer put it in Berlin in 1943.

Mere compliance would never have been enough either to smooth out all the enormous difficulties of an operation that was soon to cover the whole of Nazi-occupied and Nazi-allied Europe or to soothe the consciences of the operators, who, after all, had been brought up on the commandment 'Thou shalt not kill,' and who knew the verse from the Bible, 'Thou hast murdered and thou hast inherited,' that the judgment of the District Court of Jerusalem quoted so appropriately. What Eichmann called the 'death whirl' that descended upon Germany after the immense losses at Stalingrad – the saturation bombing of German cities, his stock excuse for killing civilians and still the stock excuse offered in Germany for the massacres – making an everyday experience of sights different from the atrocities reported at Jerusalem but no less horrible, might have contributed to the easing, or, rather, to the extinguishing, of conscience, had any conscience been left when it occurred, but according to the evidence such was not the case. The extermination machinery had been planned and perfected in all its details long before the horror of war struck Germany herself, and its intricate bureaucracy functioned with the same unwavering precision in the years of easy victory as in those last years of predictable defeat. Defections from the ranks of the ruling élite and notably from among the Higher SS officers hardly occurred at the beginning, when people might still have had a conscience; they made themselves felt only when it had become obvious that Germany was going to lose the war. Moreover, such defections were never serious enough to throw the machinery out of gear; they consisted of individual acts not of mercy but of corruption, and they were inspired not by conscience but by the desire to salt some money or some connections away for the dark days to come. Himmler's order in the fall of 1944 to halt the extermination and to dismantle the installations at the death factories sprang from his absurd but sincere conviction that the Allied powers would know how to appreciate this obliging gesture; he told a rather incredulous Eichmann that on the strength of it he would be able to negotiate a *Hubertusburger-Frieden* – an allusion to the Peace Treaty of Hubertusburg that concluded the Seven Years' War of Frederick II of Prussia in 1763 and enabled Prussia to retain Silesia, although she had lost the war.

As Eichmann told it, the most potent factor in the soothing of his own conscience was the simple fact that he could see no one, no one at all, who actually was against the Final Solution. He did encounter one exception, however, which he mentioned several times, and which must have made a deep impression on him. This happened in Hungary when he was negotiating with Dr Kastner over Himmler's offer to release one million Jews in exchange for ten thousand trucks. Kastner, apparently emboldened by the new turn of affairs, had asked Eichmann to stop 'the death mills at Auschwitz', and Eichmann had answered that he would do it 'with the greatest pleasure' (*herzlich gern*) but that, alas, it was outside his competence and outside the competence of his superiors – as indeed it was. Of course, he did not expect the Jews to share the general enthusiasm over their destruction, but he did expect more than compliance, he expected – and received, to a truly extraordinary degree – their cooperation. This was 'of course the very cornerstone' of everything he did, as it had been the very cornerstone of his activities in Vienna. Without Jewish help in administrative and police work – the final rounding up of Jews in Berlin was, as I have mentioned, done entirely by Jewish police – there would have been either complete chaos or an impossibly severe drain on German manpower. ('There can be no doubt that, without the cooperation of the victims, it would hardly have been possible for a few thousand people, most of whom, moreover, worked in offices, to liquidate many hundreds of thousands of other people ... Over the whole way to their deaths the Polish Jews got to see hardly more than a handful of Germans.' Thus R. Pendorf in the publication mentioned above. To an even greater extent this applies to those Jews who were transported to Poland to find their deaths there.) Hence, the establishing of Quisling governments in occupied territories was always accompanied by the organization of a central Jewish office, and, as we shall see later, where the Nazis did not succeed in setting up a puppet government, they also failed to enlist the cooperation of the Jews. But whereas the members of the Quisling governments were usually taken from the opposition parties, the members of the Jewish Councils were as a rule the locally recognized Jewish leaders, to whom the Nazis gave enormous powers – until they, too, were deported, to Theresienstadt or Bergen-Belsen, if they happened to be from Central or Western Europe, to Auschwitz if they were from an Eastern European community.

To a Jew this role of the Jewish leaders in the destruction of their own people is undoubtedly the darkest chapter of the whole dark story. It had been known about before, but it has now been exposed for the first time in all its pathetic and sordid detail by Raul Hilberg, whose standard work *The Destruction of the European Jews* I mentioned before. In the matter of cooperation, there was no distinction between the highly assimilated Jewish communities of Central and Western Europe and the Yiddish-speaking masses of the East. In Amsterdam as in Warsaw, in Berlin as in Budapest, Jewish officials could be trusted to compile the lists of persons and of their property, to secure money from the deportees to defray the expenses of their deportation and extermination, to keep track of vacated apartments, to supply police forces to help seize Jews and get them on trains, until, as a last gesture, they handed over the assets of the Jewish community in good order for final confiscation. They distributed the Yellow Star badges, and sometimes, as in Warsaw, 'the sale of the armbands became a regular business; there were ordinary armbands of cloth and fancy plastic armbands which were washable'. In the Nazi-inspired, but not Nazi-dictated, manifestos they issued, we still can sense how they enjoyed their new power – 'The Central Jewish Council has been granted the right of absolute disposal over all Jewish spiritual and material wealth and over all Jewish manpower,' as the first announcement of the Budapest Council phrased it. We know how the Jewish officials felt when they became instruments of murder – like captains 'whose ships were about to sink and who succeeded in bringing them safe to port by casting overboard a great part of their precious cargo'; like saviours who 'with a hundred victims save a thousand people, with a thousand ten thousand'. The truth was even more gruesome. Dr Kastner, in Hungary, for instance, saved exactly 1,684 people with approximately 476,000 victims. In order not to leave the selection to 'blind fate', 'truly holy principles' were needed 'as the guiding force of the weak human hand which puts down on paper the name of the unknown person and with this decides his life or death'. And whom did these 'holy principles' single out for salvation? Those 'who had worked all their lives for the *zibur* [community]' – i.e., the functionaries – and the 'most prominent Jews', as Kastner says in his report.

No one bothered to swear the Jewish officials to secrecy; they were voluntary 'bearers of secrets', either in order to assure quiet and prevent panic, as in Dr Kastner's case, or out of 'humane' considerations, such as that 'living in the expectation of death by gassing would only be the harder', as in the case of Dr Leo Baeck, former Chief Rabbi of Berlin. During the Eichmann trial, one witness pointed out the unfortunate consequences of this kind of 'humanity' – people volunteered for deportation from Theresienstadt to Auschwitz and denounced those who tried to tell them the truth as being 'not sane'. We know the physiognomies of the Jewish leaders during the Nazi period very well; they ranged all the way from Chaim Rumkowski, Eldest of the Jews in Lódz, called Chaim I, who issued currency notes bearing his signature and postage stamps engraved with his portrait, and who rode around in a broken-down horse-drawn carriage; through Leo Baeck, scholarly, mild-mannered, highly educated, who believed Jewish policemen would be 'more gentle and helpful' and would 'make the ordeal easier' (whereas in fact they were, of course, more brutal and less corruptible, since so much more was at stake for them); to finally, a few who committed suicide – like Adam Czerniakow, chairman of the Warsaw Jewish Council, who was not a rabbi but an unbeliever, a Polish-speaking Jewish engineer, but who must still have remembered the rabbinical saying: 'Let them kill you, but don't cross the line.'

That the prosecution in Jerusalem, so careful not to embarrass the Adenauer administration, should have avoided, with even greater and more obvious justification, bringing this chapter of the story into the open was almost a matter of course. (These issues, however, are discussed quite openly and with astonishing frankness in Israeli schoolbooks – as may conveniently be gathered from the article 'Young Israelis and Jews Abroad – A Study of Selected History Textbooks' by Mark M. Krug, in *Comparative Education Review*, October 1963.) The chapter must be included here, however, because it accounts for certain otherwise inexplicable lacunae in the documentation of a generally over-documented case. The judges mentioned one such instance, the absence of H. G. Adler's book *Theresienstadt 1941–1945* (1955), which the prosecution, in some embarrassment, admitted to be 'authentic, based on irrefutable sources'. The reason for the omission was clear. The book describes in detail how the feared 'transport lists' were put together by the Jewish Council of Theresienstadt after the SS had given some general directives, stipulating how many should be sent away, and of what age, sex, profession, and country of origin. The prosecution's case would have been weakened if it had been forced to admit that the naming of individuals who were sent to their doom had been, with few exceptions, the job of the Jewish administration. And the Deputy State Attorney, Mr

Ya'akov Baror, who handled the intervention from the bench, in a way indicated this when he said: 'I am trying to bring out those things which somehow refer to the accused without damaging the picture in its entirety.' The picture would indeed have been greatly damaged by the inclusion of Adler's book, since it would have contradicted testimony given by the chief witness on Theresienstadt, who claimed that Eichmann himself had made these individual selections. Even more important, the prosecution's general picture of a clear-cut division between persecutors and victims would have suffered greatly. To make available evidence that does not support the case for the prosecution is usually the job of the defence, and the question why Dr Servatius, who perceived some minor inconsistencies in the testimony, did not avail himself of such easily obtainable and widely known documentation is difficult to answer. He could have pointed to the fact that Eichmann, immediately upon being transformed from an expert in emigration into an expert in 'evacuation', appointed his old Jewish associates in the emigration business – Dr Paul Eppstein, who had been in charge of emigration in Berlin, and Rabbi Benjamin Murmelstein, who had held the same job in Vienna – as 'Jewish Elders' in Theresienstadt. This would have done more to demonstrate the atmosphere in which Eichmann worked than all the unpleasant and often downright offensive talk about oaths, loyalty, and the virtues of unquestioning obedience.

The testimony of Mrs Charlotte Salzberger on Theresienstadt, from which I quoted above, permitted us to cast at least a glance into this neglected corner of what the prosecution kept calling the 'general picture'. The presiding judge did not like the term and he did not like the picture. He told the Attorney General several times that 'we are not drawing pictures here', that there is 'an indictment and this indictment is the framework for our trial', that the court 'has its own view about this trial, according to the indictment', and that 'the prosecution must adjust to what the court lays down' – admirable admonitions for criminal proceedings, none of which was heeded. The prosecution did worse than not heed them, it simply refused to guide its witnesses – or, if the court became too insistent, it asked a few haphazard questions, very casually – with the result that the witnesses behaved as though they were speakers at a meeting chaired by the Attorney General, who introduced them to the audience before they took the floor. They could talk almost as long as they wished, and it was a rare occasion when they were asked a specific question.

This atmosphere, not of a show trial but of a mass meeting, at which speaker after speaker does his best to arouse the audience, was especially noticeable when the prosecution called witness after witness to testify to the rising in the Warsaw ghetto and to the similar attempts in Vilna and Kovno – matters that had no connection whatever with the crimes of the accused. The testimony of these people would have contributed something to the trial if they had told of the activities of the Jewish Councils, which had played such a great and disastrous role in their own heroic efforts. Of course, there was some mention of this – witnesses speaking of 'SS men and their helpers' pointed out that they counted among the latter the 'ghetto police which was also an instrument in the hands of the Nazi murderers' as well as 'the *Judenrat*' – but they were only too glad not to 'elaborate' on this side of their story, and they shifted the discussion to the role of real traitors, of whom there were few, and who were 'nameless people, unknown to the Jewish public', such as 'all undergrounds which fought against the Nazis suffered from'. (The audience while these witnesses testified had changed again; it consisted now of *Kibbuzniks*, members of the Israeli communal settlements to which the speakers belonged.) The purest and clearest account came from Zivia Lubetkin Zuckerman, today a woman of perhaps forty, still very beautiful, completely free of sentimentality or self-indulgence, her facts well organized, and always quite sure of the point she wished to make. Legally, the testimony of these witnesses was immaterial – Mr Hausner did not mention one of them in his last *plaidoyer* – except insofar as it constituted proof of close contacts between Jewish partisans and the Polish and Russian underground fighters, which, apart from contradicting other testimony ('We had the whole population against us'), could have been useful to the defence, since it offered much better justification for the wholesale slaughter of civilians than Eichmann's repeated claim that 'Weizmann had declared war on Germany in 1939.' (This was sheer nonsense. All that Chaim Weizmann had said, at the close of the last prewar Zionist Congress, was that the war of the Western democracies 'is our war, their struggle is our struggle'. The tragedy, as Hausner rightly pointed out, was precisely that the Jews were not recognized by the

Nazis as belligerents, for if they had been they would
have survived, in prisoner-of-war or civilian internment
camps.) Had Dr Servatius made this point, the prosecution would have been forced to admit how pitifully
small these resistance groups had been, how incredibly
weak and essentially harmless – and, moreover, how
little they had represented the Jewish population, who
at one point even took arms against them.

While the legal irrelevance of all this very time-
consuming testimony remained pitifully clear, the political intention of the Israeli government in introducing
it was also not difficult to guess. Mr Hausner (or Mr
Ben-Gurion) probably wanted to demonstrate that whatever resistance there had been had come from Zionists,
as though, of all Jews, only the Zionists knew that if you
could not save your life it might still be worth while to
save your honour, as Mr Zuckerman put it; that the
worst that could happen to the human person under
such circumstances was to be and to remain 'innocent',
as became clear from the tenor and drift of Mrs Zuckerman's testimony. However, these 'political' intentions
misfired, for the witnesses were truthful and told the
court that all Jewish organizations and parties had played
their role in the resistance, so the true distinction was
not between Zionists and non-Zionists but between
organized and unorganized people, and, even more
important, between the young and the middle-aged.
To be sure, those who resisted were a minority, a tiny
minority, but under the circumstances 'the miracle was',
as one of them pointed out, 'that this minority existed'.

Legal considerations aside, the appearance in the witness box of the former Jewish resistance fighters was welcome enough. It dissipated the haunting spectre of universal cooperation, the stifling, poisoned atmosphere which had surrounded the Final Solution. The well-known fact that the actual work of killing in the extermination centres was usually in the hands of Jewish commandos had been fairly and squarely established by witnesses for the prosecution – how they had worked in the gas chambers and the crematories, how they had pulled the gold teeth and cut the hair of the corpses, how they had dug the graves and, later, dug them up again to extinguish the traces of mass murder; how Jewish technicians had built gas chambers in Theresienstadt, where the Jewish 'autonomy' had been carried so far that even the hangman was a Jew. But this was only horrible, it was no moral problem. The selection and classification of workers in the camps was made by the SS, who had a marked predilection for the criminal elements; and, anyhow, it could only have been the selection of the worst. (This was especially true in Poland, where the Nazis had exterminated a large proportion of the Jewish intelligentsia at the same time that they killed Polish intellectuals and members of the professions – in marked contrast, incidentally, to their policy in Western Europe, where they tended to save prominent Jews in order to exchange them for German civilian internees or prisoners of war; Bergen-Belsen was originally a camp for 'exchange Jews'.) The moral problem lay in the amount of truth there was in Eichmann's description of Jewish cooperation, even under the conditions of the Final Solution: 'The formation of the

Jewish Council [at Theresienstadt] and the distribution of business was left to the discretion of the Council, except for the appointment of the president, who the president was to be, which depended upon us, of course. However, this appointment was not in the form of a dictatorial decision. The functionaries with whom we were in constant contact – well, they had to be treated with kid gloves. They were not ordered around, for the simple reason that if the chief officials had been told what to do in the form of: you must, you have to, that would not have helped matters any. If the person in question does not like what he is doing, the whole works will suffer ... We did our best to make everything somehow palatable.' No doubt they did; the problem is how it was possible for them to succeed.

Thus, the gravest omission from the 'general picture' was that of a witness to testify to the cooperation between the Nazi rulers and the Jewish authorities, and hence of an opportunity to raise the question: 'Why did you cooperate in the destruction of your own people and, eventually, in your own ruin?' The only witness who had been a prominent member of a *Judenrat* was Pinchas Freudiger, the former Baron Philip von Freudiger, of Budapest, and during his testimony the only serious incidents in the audience took place; people screamed at the witness in Hungarian and in Yiddish, and the court had to interrupt the session. Freudiger, an Orthodox Jew of considerable dignity, was shaken: 'There are people here who say they were not told to escape. But fifty per cent of the people who escaped were captured and killed' – as compared with ninety-nine per cent, for those who did not escape. 'Where could they have gone to? Where could they have fled?' – but he himself fled, to Rumania, because he was rich and Wisliceny helped him. 'What could we have done? What could we have done?' And the only response to this came from the presiding judge: 'I do not think this is an answer to the question' – a question raised by the gallery but not by the court.

The matter of cooperation was twice mentioned by the judges; Judge Yitzak Raveh elicited from one of the resistance witnesses an admission that the 'ghetto police' were an 'instrument in the hands of murderers' and an acknowledgement of 'the *Judenrat*'s policy of cooperating with the Nazis'; and Judge Halevi found out from Eichmann in cross-examination that the Nazis had regarded this cooperation as the very cornerstone of their Jewish policy. But the question the prosecutor regularly addressed to each witness except the resistance fighters which sounded so very natural to those who knew nothing of the factual background of the trial, the question 'Why did you not rebel?' actually served as a smoke screen for the question that was not asked. And thus it came to pass that all answers to the unanswerable question Mr Hausner put to his witnesses were considerably less than 'the truth, the whole truth, and nothing but the truth'. True it was that the Jewish people as a whole had not been organized, that they had possessed no territory, no government, and no army, that, in the hour of their greatest need, they had no government-in-exile to represent them among the Allies (the Jewish Agency for Palestine, under Dr Weizmann's presidency, was at best a miserable substitute), no caches of weapons, no youth with military training. But the whole truth was that there existed Jewish community organizations and Jewish party and welfare organizations on both the local and the international level. Wherever Jews lived, there were recognized Jewish leaders, and this leadership, almost without exception, cooperated in one way or another, for one reason or another, with the Nazis. The whole truth was that if the Jewish people had really been unorganized and leaderless, there would have been chaos and plenty of misery but the total number of victims would hardly have been between four and a half and six million people. (According to Freudiger's calculations about half of them could have saved themselves if they had not followed the instructions of the Jewish Councils. This is of course a mere estimate, which, however, oddly jibes with the rather reliable figures we have from Holland and which I owe to Dr L. de Jong, the head of the Netherlands State Institute for War Documentation. In Holland, where the *Joodsche Raad* like all the Dutch authorities very quickly became an 'instrument of the Nazis', 103,000 Jews were deported to the death camps and some five thousand to Theresienstadt in the usual way, i.e., with the cooperation of the Jewish Council. Only five hundred and nineteen Jews returned from the death camps. In contrast to this figure, ten thousand of those twenty to twenty-five thousand Jews who escaped the Nazis – and that meant also the Jewish Council – and went underground survived; again forty to fifty per cent. Most of the Jews sent to Theresienstadt returned to Holland.)

I have dwelt on this chapter of the story, which the

Jerusalem trial failed to put before the eyes of the world in its true dimensions, because it offers the most striking insight into the totality of the moral collapse the Nazis caused in respectable European society – not only in Germany but in almost all countries, not only among the persecutors but also among the victims. Eichmann, in contrast to other elements in the Nazi movement, had always been overawed by 'good society', and the politeness he often showed to German-speaking Jewish functionaries was to a large extent the result of his recognition that he was dealing with people who were socially his superiors. He was not at all, as one witness called him, a '*Landsknechtnatur*', a mercenary, who wanted to escape to regions where there aren't no Ten Commandments an' a man can raise a thirst. What he fervently believed in up to the end was success, the chief standard of 'good society' as he knew it. Typical was his last word on the subject of Hitler – whom he and his comrade Sassen had agreed to 'shirr out' of their story; Hitler, he said, 'may have been wrong all down the line, but one thing is beyond dispute: the man was able to work his way up from lance corporal in the German Army to Führer of a people of almost eighty million . . . His success alone proved to me that I should subordinate myself to this man.' His conscience was indeed set at rest when he saw the zeal and eagerness with which 'good society' everywhere reacted as he did. He did not need to 'close his ears to the voice of conscience', as the judgment has it, not because he had none, but because his conscience spoke with a 'respectable voice', with the voice of respectable society around him.

That there were no voices from the outside to arouse his conscience was one of Eichmann's points, and it was the task of the prosecution to prove that this was not so, that there were voices he could have listened to, and that, anyhow, he had done his work with a zeal far beyond the call of duty. Which turned out to be true enough, except that, strange as it may appear, his murderous zeal was not altogether unconnected with the ambiguity in the voices of those who at one time or another tried to restrain him. We need mention here only in passing the so-called 'inner emigration' in Germany – those people who frequently had held positions, even high ones, in the Third Reich and who, after the end of the war, told themselves and the world at large that they had always been 'inwardly opposed' to the regime. The question here is not whether or not they are telling the truth; the point is, rather, that no secret in the secret-ridden atmosphere of the Hitler regime was better kept than such 'inward opposition'. This was almost a matter of course under the conditions of Nazi terror; as a rather well-known 'inner emigrant', who certainly believed in his own sincerity, once told me, they had to appear 'outwardly' even more like Nazis than ordinary Nazis did, in order to keep their secret. (This, incidentally, may explain why the few known protests against the extermination programme came not from the Army commanders but from old Party members.) Hence, the only possible way to live in the Third Reich and not act as a Nazi was not to appear at all: 'Withdrawal from significant participation in public life' was indeed the only criterion by which one might have measured individual guilt, as Otto Kirchheimer recently remarked in his *Political Justice* (1961). If the term was to make any sense, the 'inner emigrant' could only be one who lived 'as though outcast among his own people amidst blindly believing masses', as Professor Hermann Jahrreiss pointed out in his 'Statement for All Defence Attorneys' before the Nuremberg Tribunal. For opposition was indeed 'utterly pointless' in the absence of all organization. It is true that there were Germans who lived for twelve years in this 'outer cold', but their number was insignificant, even among the members of the resistance. In recent years, the slogan of the 'inner emigration' (the term itself has a definitely equivocal flavour, as it can mean either an emigration into the inward regions of one's soul or a way of conducting oneself as though he were an emigrant) has become a sort of a joke. The sinister Dr Otto Bradfisch, former member of one of the *Einsatzgruppen*, who presided over the killing of at least fifteen thousand people, told a German court that he had always been 'inwardly opposed' to what he was doing. Perhaps the death of fifteen thousand people was necessary to provide him with an alibi in the eyes of 'true Nazis'. (The same argument was advanced, though with considerably less success, in a Polish court by former Gauleiter Arthur Greiser of the Warthegau: only his 'official soul' had carried out the crimes for which he was hanged in 1946, his 'private soul' had always been against them.)

While Eichmann may never have encountered an 'inner emigrant', he must have been well acquainted with many of those numerous civil servants who today assert that they stayed in their jobs for no other reason than to 'mitigate' matters and to prevent 'real Nazis' from taking over their posts. We mentioned the famous case of Dr Hans Globke, Undersecretary of State and from 1953 to 1963 chief of the personnel division in the West German Chancellery. Since he was the only civil servant in this category to be mentioned during the trial, it may be worth while to look into his mitigating activities. Dr Globke had been employed in the Prussian Ministry of the Interior before Hitler's rise to power, and had shown there a rather premature interest in the Jewish question. He formulated the first of the directives in which 'proof of Aryan descent' was demanded, in this case of persons who applied for permission to change their names. This circular letter of December 1932 – issued at a time when Hitler's rise to power was not yet a certainty, but a strong probability – oddly anticipated the 'top secret decrees', that is, the typically totalitarian rule by means of laws that are not brought to the attention of the public, which the Hitler regime introduced much later, in notifying the recipients that 'these directives are not for publication'. Dr Globke, as I have mentioned, kept his interest in names, and since it is true that his Commentary on the Nuremberg Laws of 1935 was considerably harsher than the earlier interpretation of *Rassenschande* by the Ministry of the Interior's expert on Jewish affairs, Dr Bernhard Lösener, an old member of the Party, one could even accuse him of having made things worse than they were under 'real Nazis'. But even if we were to grant him all his good intentions, it is hard indeed to see what he could have done under the circumstances to make things better than they would otherwise have been. Recently, however, a German newspaper, after much searching, came up with an answer to this puzzling question. They found a document, duly signed by Dr Globke, which decreed that Czech brides of German soldiers had to furnish photographs of themselves in bathing suits in order to obtain a marriage licence. And Dr Globke explained: 'With this confidential ordinance a three-year-old scandal was somewhat *mitigated*'; for until his intervention, Czech brides had to furnish snapshots that showed them stark naked.

Dr Globke, as he explained at Nuremberg, was fortunate in that he worked under the orders of another 'mitigator', Staatssekretär (Undersecretary of State) Wilhelm Stuckart, whom we met as one of the eager members of the Wannsee Conference. Stuckart's attenuation activities concerned half-Jews, whom he proposed to sterilize. (The Nuremberg court, in possession of the minutes of the Wannsee Conference, may not have believed that he had known nothing of the extermination programme, but it sentenced him to time served on account of ill health. A German denazification court fined him five hundred marks and declared him a 'nominal member of the Party' – a *Mitläufer* – although they must have known at least that Stuckart belonged to the 'old guard' of the Party and had joined the SS early, as an honorary member.) Clearly, the story of the 'mitigators' in Hitler's offices belongs among the postwar fairy tales, and we can dismiss them, too, as voices that might possibly have reached Eichmann's conscience.

The question of these voices became serious, in Jerusalem, with the appearance in court of Propst Heinrich

Grüber, a Protestant minister, who had come to the trial as the only German (and, incidentally, except for Judge Michael Musmanno from the United States, the only non-Jewish) witness for the prosecution. (German witnesses for the defence were excluded from the outset, since they would have exposed themselves to arrest and prosecution in Israel under the same law as that under which Eichmann was tried.) Propst Grüber had belonged to the numerically small and politically irrelevant group of persons who were opposed to Hitler on principle, and not out of nationalist considerations, and whose stand on the Jewish question had been without equivocation. He promised to be a splendid witness, since Eichmann had negotiated with him several times, and his mere appearance in the courtroom created a kind of sensation. Unfortunately, his testimony was vague; he did not remember, after so many years, when he had spoken with Eichmann, or, and this was more serious, on what subjects. All he recalled clearly was that he had once asked for unleavened bread to be shipped to Hungary for Passover, and that he had travelled to Switzerland during the war to tell his Christian friends how dangerous the situation was and to urge that more opportunities for emigration be provided. (The negotiations must have taken place prior to the implementing of the Final Solution, which coincided with Himmler's decree forbidding all emigration; they probably occurred before the invasion of Russia.) He got his unleavened bread, and he got safely to Switzerland and back again. His troubles started later, when the deportations had begun. Propst Grüber and his group of Protestant clergymen first intervened merely 'on behalf of people who had been wounded in the course of the First World War and of those who had been awarded high military decorations; on behalf of the old and on behalf of the widows of those killed in World War I'. These categories corresponded to those that had originally been exempted by the Nazis themselves. Now Grüber was told that what he was doing 'ran counter to the policy of the government', but nothing serious happened to him. But shortly after this, Propst Grüber did something really extraordinary: he tried to reach the concentration camp of Gurs, in southern France, where Vichy France had interned, together with German Jewish refugees, some seventy-five hundred Jews from Baden and the Saarpfalz whom Eichmann had smuggled across the German–French border in the fall of 1940, and who, according to Propst Grüber's information, were even worse off than the Jews deported to Poland. The result of this attempt was that he was arrested and put in a concentration camp – first in Sachsenhausen and then in Dachau. (A similar fate befell the Catholic priest Dompropst Bernard Lichtenberg, of St Hedwig's Cathedral in Berlin; he not only had dared to pray publicly for all Jews, baptized or not – which was considerably more dangerous than to intervene for 'special cases' – but he had also demanded that he be allowed to join the Jews on their journey to the East. He died on his way to a concentration camp.)

Apart from testifying to the existence of 'another Germany', Propst Grüber did not contribute much to either the legal or the historical significance of the trial. He was full of pat judgments about Eichmann – he was like 'a block of ice', like 'marble', a *'Landsknechtsnatur'*, a 'bicycle rider' (a current German idiom for someone who kowtows to his superiors and kicks his subordinates) – none of which showed him as a particularly good psychologist, quite apart from the fact that the 'bicycle rider' charge was contradicted by evidence which showed Eichmann to have been rather decent toward his subordinates. Anyway, these were interpretations and conclusions that would normally have been stricken from any court record – though in Jerusalem they even found their way into the judgment. Without them Propst Grüber's testimony could have strengthened the case for the defence, for Eichmann had never given Grüber a direct answer, he had always told him to come back, as he had to ask for further instructions. More important, Dr Servatius for once took the initiative and asked the witness a highly pertinent question: 'Did you try to influence him? Did you, as a clergyman, try to appeal to his feelings, preach to him, and tell him that his conduct was contrary to morality?' Of course, the very courageous Propst had done nothing of the sort, and his answers now were highly embarrassing. He said that 'deeds are more effective than words', and that 'words would have been useless'; he spoke in clichés that had nothing to do with the reality of the situation, where 'mere words' would have been deeds, and where it had perhaps been the duty of a clergyman to test the 'uselessness of words'.

Even more pertinent than Dr Servatius' question was what Eichmann said about this episode in his last statement: 'Nobody,' he repeated, 'came to me and reproached me for anything in the performance of my duties. Not even Pastor Grüber claims to have done so.' He then added: 'He came to me and sought alleviation of suffering, but did not actually object to the very performance of my duties as such.' From Propst Grüber's own testimony, it appeared that he sought not so much 'alleviation of suffering' as exemptions from it, in accordance with well-established categories recognized earlier by the Nazis. The categories had been accepted without protest by German Jewry from the very beginning. And the acceptance of privileged categories – German Jews as against Polish Jews, war veterans and decorated Jews as against ordinary Jews, families whose ancestors were German-born as against recently naturalized citizens, etc. – had been the beginning of the moral collapse of respectable Jewish society. (In view of the fact that today such matters are often treated as though there existed a law of human nature compelling everybody to lose his dignity in the face of disaster, we may recall the attitude of the French Jewish war veterans who were offered the same privileges by their government, and replied: 'We solemnly declare that we renounce any exceptional benefits we may derive from our status as ex-servicemen' (*American Jewish Yearbook*, 1945).) Needless to say, the Nazis themselves never took these distinctions seriously, for them a Jew was a Jew, but the categories played a certain role up to the very end, since they helped put to rest a certain uneasiness among the German population: only Polish Jews were deported, only people who had shirked military service, and so on. For those who did not want to close their eyes it must have been clear from the beginning that it 'was a general practice to allow certain exceptions in order to be able to maintain the general rule all the more easily' (in the words of Louis de Jong in an illuminating article on 'Jews and Non-Jews in Nazi-Occupied Holland').

What was morally so disastrous in the acceptance of these privileged categories was that everyone who demanded to have an 'exception' made in his case implicitly recognized the rule, but this point, apparently, was never grasped by these 'good men', Jewish and Gentile, who busied themselves about all those 'special cases' for which preferential treatment could be asked. The extent to which even the Jewish victims had accepted the standards of the Final Solution is perhaps nowhere more glaringly evident than in the so-called Kastner Report (available in German, *Der Kastner-Bericht über Eichmanns Menschenhandel in Ungarn,* 1961). Even after the end of the war, Kastner was proud of his success in saving 'prominent Jews', a category officially introduced by the Nazis in 1942, as though in his view, too, it went without saying that a famous Jew had more right to stay alive than an ordinary one; to take upon himself such 'responsibilities' – to help the Nazis in their efforts to pick out 'famous' people from the anonymous mass, for this is what it amounted to – 'required more courage than to face death'. But if the Jewish and Gentile pleaders of 'special cases' were unaware of their involuntary complicity, this implicit recognition of the rule, which spelled death for all non-special cases, must have been very obvious to those who were engaged in the business of murder. They must have felt, at least, that by being asked to make exceptions, and by occasionally granting them, and thus earning gratitude, they had convinced their opponents of the lawfulness of what they were doing.

Moreover, Propst Grüber and the Jerusalem court were quite mistaken in assuming that requests for exemptions originated only with opponents of the regime. On the contrary, as Heydrich explicitly stated during the Wannsee Conference, the establishment of Theresienstadt as a ghetto for privileged categories was prompted by the great number of such interventions from all sides. Theresienstadt later became a showplace for visitors from abroad and served to deceive the outside world, but this was not its original *raison d'être*. The horrible thinning-out process that regularly occurred in this 'paradise' – 'distinguished from other camps as day is from night', as Eichmann rightly remarked – was necessary because there was never enough room to provide for all who were privileged, and we know from a directive issued by Ernst Kaltenbrunner, head of the RSHA, that 'special care was taken not to deport Jews with connections and important acquaintances in the outside world.' In other words, the less 'prominent' Jews were constantly sacrificed to those whose disappearance in the East would create unpleasant inquiries. The 'acquaintances in the outside world' did not necessarily live outside Germany; according to Himmler, there were 'eighty million good Germans, each of whom has his decent Jew. It is clear, the others are pigs, but this particular Jew is first-rate' (Hilberg). Hitler himself is said to have known three hundred and forty 'first-rate Jews', whom he had either altogether assimilated to the status of Germans or granted the privileges of half-Jews. Thousands of half-Jews had been exempted from all restrictions, which might explain Heydrich's role in the SS and Generalfeldmarschall Erhard Milch's role in Göring's Air Force, for it was generally known that Heydrich and Milch were half-Jews. (Among the major war criminals, only two repented in the face of death: Heydrich, during the nine days it took him to die from the wounds inflicted by Czech patriots, and Hans Frank in his death cell at Nuremberg. It is an uncomfortable fact, for it is difficult not to suspect that what Heydrich at least repented of was not murder but that he had betrayed his own people.) If interventions on behalf of 'prominent' Jews came from 'prominent' people, they often were quite successful. Thus Sven Hedin, one of Hitler's most ardent admirers, intervened for a well-known geographer, a Professor Philippsohn of Bonn, who was 'living under undignified conditions at Theresienstadt'; in a letter to Hitler, Hedin threatened that 'his attitude to Germany would be dependent upon Philippsohn's fate', whereupon (according to H. G. Adler's book on Theresienstadt) Mr Philippsohn was promptly provided with better quarters.

In Germany today, this notion of 'prominent' Jews has not yet been forgotten. While the veterans and other privileged groups are no longer mentioned, the fate of 'famous' Jews is still deplored at the expense of all others. There are more than a few people, especially among the cultural élite, who still publicly regret the fact that Germany sent Einstein packing, without realizing that it was a much greater crime to kill little Hans Cohn from around the corner, even though he was no genius.

Execution

[. . .] The proceedings before the Court of Appeal lasted only a week, after which the court adjourned for two months. On May 29, 1962, the second judgment was read – somewhat less voluminous than the first, but still fifty-one single-spaced legal-sized pages. It ostensibly confirmed the District Court on all points, and to make this confirmation the judges would not have needed two months and fifty-one pages. The judgment of the Court of Appeal was actually a revision of the judgment of the lower court, although it did not say so. In conspicuous contrast to the original judgment, it was now found that 'the appellant had received no "superior orders" at all. He was his own superior, and he gave all orders in matters that concerned Jewish affairs'; he had, moreover, 'eclipsed in importance all his superiors, including Müller'. And, in reply to the obvious argument of the defence that the Jews would have been no better off had Eichmann never existed, the judges now stated that 'the idea of the Final Solution would never have assumed the infernal forms of the flayed skin and tortured flesh of millions of Jews without the fanatical zeal and the unquenchable blood thirst of the appellant and his accomplices.' Israel's Supreme Court had not only accepted the arguments of the prosecution, it had adopted its very language.

The same day, 29 May, Itzhak Ben-Zvi, President of Israel, received Eichmann's plea for mercy, four hand-written pages, made 'upon instructions of my counsel', together with letters from his wife and his family in Linz. The President also received hundreds of letters and telegrams from all over the world, pleading for clemency; outstanding among the senders were the Central Conference of American Rabbis, the representative body of Reform Judaism in this country, and a group of professors from the Hebrew University in Jerusalem, headed by Martin Buber, who had been opposed to the trial from the start, and who now tried to persuade Ben-Gurion to intervene for clemency. Mr Ben-Zvi rejected all pleas for mercy on 31 May, two days after the Supreme Court had delivered its judgment, and a few hours later on that same day – it was a Thursday – shortly before midnight, Eichmann was hanged, his body was cremated, and the ashes were scattered in the Mediterranean outside Israeli waters.

The speed with which the death sentence was carried out was extraordinary, even if one takes into account that Thursday night was the last possible occasion before the following Monday, since Friday, Saturday, and Sunday are all religious holidays for one or another of the three denominations in the country. The execution took place less than two hours after Eichmann was informed of the rejection of his plea for mercy; there had not even been time for a last meal. The explanation may well be found in two last-minute attempts Dr Servatius made to save his client – an application to a court in West Germany to force the government to demand Eichmann's extradition, even now, and a threat to invoke Article 25 of the Convention for the Protection of Human Rights and Fundamental Freedoms. Neither Dr Servatius nor his assistant was in Israel when Eichmann's plea was rejected, and the Israeli government probably wanted to close the case, which had been going on for two years, before the defence could even apply for a stay in the date of execution.

The death sentence had been expected, and there was hardly anyone to quarrel with it; but things were altogether different when it was learned that the Israelis had carried it out. The protests were short-lived, but they were widespread and they were voiced by people of influence and prestige. The most common argument was that Eichmann's deeds defied the possibility of human punishment, that it was pointless to impose the death sentence for crimes of such magnitude – which, of course, was true, in a sense, except that it could not conceivably mean that he who had murdered millions should for this very reason escape punishment. On a considerably lower level, the death sentence was called 'unimaginative', and very imaginative alternatives were proposed forthwith – Eichmann 'should have spent the rest of his life at hard labour in the arid stretches of the Negev, helping with his sweat to reclaim the Jewish homeland', a punishment he would probably not have survived for more than a single day, to say nothing of the fact that in Israel the desert of the south is hardly looked upon as a penal colony; or, in Madison Avenue style, Israel should have reached 'divine heights', rising above 'the understandable, legal, political, and even human considerations', by calling together 'all those who took part in the capture, trial, and sentencing to a public ceremony, with Eichmann there in shackles, and with television cameras and radio to decorate them as the heroes of the century'.

Martin Buber called the execution a 'mistake of historical dimensions', as it might 'serve to expiate the guilt felt by many young persons in Germany' – an argument that oddly echoed Eichmann's own ideas on the matter, though Buber hardly knew that he had wanted to hang himself in public in order to lift the burden of guilt from the shoulders of German youngsters. (It is strange that Buber, a man not only of eminence but of very great intelligence, should not see how spurious these much publicized guilt feelings necessarily are. It is quite gratifying to feel guilty if you haven't done anything wrong: how noble! Whereas it is rather hard and certainly depressing to admit guilt and to repent. The youth of Germany is surrounded, on all sides and in all walks of life, by men in positions of authority and in public office who are very guilty indeed but who *feel* nothing of the sort. The normal reaction to this state of affairs should be indignation, but indignation would be quite risky – not a danger to life and limb but definitely a handicap in a career. Those young German men and women who every once in a while – on the occasion of all the *Diary of Anne Frank* hubbub and of the Eichmann trial – treat us to hysterical outbreaks of guilt feelings are not staggering under the burden of the past, their fathers' guilt; rather, they are trying to escape from the pressure of very present and actual problems into a cheap sentimentality.)

Professor Buber went on to say that he felt 'no pity at all' for Eichmann, because he could feel pity 'only for those whose actions I understand in my heart', and he stressed what he had said many years ago in Germany – that he had 'only in a formal sense a common humanity with those who took part' in the acts of the Third Reich. This lofty attitude was, of course, more of a luxury than those who had to try Eichmann could afford, since the law presupposes precisely that we have a common humanity with those whom we accuse and judge and condemn. As far as I know, Buber was the only philosopher to go on public record on the subject of Eichmann's execution (shortly before the trial started, Karl Jaspers had given a radio interview in Basel, later published in *Der Monat*, in which he argued the case for an international tribunal); it was disappointing to find him dodging, on the highest possible level, the very problem Eichmann and his deeds had posed.

Least of all was heard from those who were against the death penalty on principle, unconditionally; their arguments would have remained valid, since they would not have needed to specify them for this particular case. They seem to have felt – rightly, I think – that this was not a very promising case on which to fight.

Adolf Eichmann went to the gallows with great dignity. He had asked for a bottle of red wine and had drunk half of it. He refused the help of the Protestant minister, the Reverend William Hull, who offered to read the Bible with him: he had only two more hours to live, and therefore no 'time to waste'. He walked the fifty yards from his cell to the execution chamber calm and erect, with his hands bound behind him. When the guards tied his ankles and knees, he asked them to loosen the bonds so that he could stand straight. 'I don't need that,' he said when the black hood was offered him. He was in complete command of himself, nay, he was more: he was completely himself. Nothing could have demonstrated this more convincingly than the grotesque silliness of his last words. He began by stating emphatically that he was a *Gottgläubiger*, to express in common Nazi fashion that he was no Christian and did not believe in life after death. He then proceeded: 'After a short while, gentlemen, *we shall all meet again*. Such is the fate of all men. Long live Germany, long live Argentina, long live Austria. *I shall not forget them.*' In the face of death, he had found the cliché used in funeral oratory. Under the gallows, his memory played him the last trick; he was 'elated' and he forgot that this was his own funeral.

It was as though in those last minutes he was summing up the lesson that this long course in human wickedness had taught us – the lesson of the fearsome, word-and-thought-defying *banality of evil*.

Epilogue

[...] In the eyes of the Jews, thinking exclusively in terms of their own history, the catastrophe that had befallen them under Hitler, in which a third of the people perished, appeared not as the most recent of crimes, the unprecedented crime of genocide, but, on the contrary, as the oldest crime they knew and remembered. This misunderstanding, almost inevitable if we consider not only the facts of Jewish history but also, and more important, the current Jewish historical self-understanding, is actually at the root of all the failures and shortcomings of the Jerusalem trial. None of the participants ever arrived at a clear understanding of the actual horror of Auschwitz, which is of a different nature from all the atrocities of the past, because it appeared to prosecution and judges alike as not much more than the most horrible pogrom in Jewish history. They therefore believed that a direct line existed from the early anti-Semitism of the Nazi Party to the Nuremberg Laws and from there to the expulsion of Jews from the Reich and, finally, to the gas chambers. Politically and legally, however, these were 'crimes' different not only in degree of seriousness but in essence.

The Nuremberg Laws of 1935 legalized the discrimination practised before that by the German majority against the Jewish minority. According to international law, it was the privilege of the sovereign German nation to declare to be a national minority whatever part of its population it saw fit, as long as its minority laws conformed to the rights and guarantees established by internationally recognized minority treaties and agreements. International Jewish organizations therefore promptly tried to obtain for this newest minority the same rights and guarantees that minorities in Eastern and Southeastern Europe had been granted at Geneva. But even though this protection was not granted, the Nuremberg Laws were generally recognized by other nations as part of German law, so that it was impossible for a German national to enter into a 'mixed marriage' in Holland, for instance. The crime of the Nuremberg Laws was a national crime; it violated national, constitutional rights and liberties, but it was of no concern to the comity of nations. 'Enforced emigration', however, or expulsion, which became official policy after 1938, did concern the international community, for the simple reason that those who were expelled appeared at the frontiers of other countries, which were forced either to accept the uninvited guests or to smuggle them into another country, equally unwilling to accept them. Expulsion of nationals, in other words, is already an offence against humanity, if by 'humanity' we understand no more than the comity of nations. Neither the national crime of legalized discrimination, which amounted to persecution by law, nor the international crime of expulsion was unprecedented, even in the modern age. Legalized discrimination had been practiced by all Balkan countries, and expulsion on a mass scale had occurred after many revolutions. It was when the Nazi regime declared that the German people not only were unwilling to have any Jews in Germany but wished to make the entire Jewish people disappear from the face of the earth that the new crime, the crime against humanity – in the sense of a crime 'against the human status', or against the very nature of mankind – appeared. Expulsion and genocide, though both are international offences, must remain distinct, the former is an offence against fellow-nations, whereas the latter is an attack upon human diversity as such, that is, upon a characteristic of the 'human status' without which the very words 'mankind' or 'humanity' would be devoid of meaning.

Had the court in Jerusalem understood that there were distinctions between discrimination, expulsion, and genocide, it would immediately have become clear that the supreme crime it was confronted with, the physical extermination of the Jewish people, was a crime against humanity, perpetrated upon the body of the Jewish people, and that only the choice of victims, not the nature of the crime, could be derived from the long history of Jew-hatred and anti-Semitism. Insofar as the victims were Jews, it was right and proper that a Jewish court should sit in judgment; but insofar as the crime was a crime against humanity, it needed an international tribunal to do justice to it. (The failure of the court to draw this distinction was surprising, because it had actually been made before by the former Israeli Minister of Justice, Mr Rosen, who in 1950 had insisted on 'a distinction between this bill [for crimes against the Jewish people] and the Law for the Prevention and Punishment of Genocide', which was discussed but not passed by the Israeli Parliament. Obviously, the court felt it had no right to overstep the limits of municipal law, so that genocide, not being covered by an Israeli law, could not properly enter into its considerations.) Among the numerous and highly qualified voices that raised objections to the court in Jerusalem and were in favour of an international tribunal, only one, that of Karl Jaspers, stated clearly and unequivocally – in a radio interview held before the trial began and later published in *Der*

Monat – that 'the crime against the Jews was also a crime against mankind', and that 'consequently the verdict can be handed down only by a court of justice representing all mankind'. Jaspers proposed that the court in Jerusalem, after hearing the factual evidence, 'waive' the right to pass sentence, declaring itself 'incompetent' to do so, because the legal nature of the crime in question was still open to dispute, as was the subsequent question of who would be competent to pass sentence on a crime which had been committed on government orders. Jaspers stated further that one thing alone was certain: 'This crime is both more and less than common murder,' and though it was not a 'war crime', either, there was no doubt that 'mankind would certainly be destroyed if states were permitted to perpetrate such crimes'.

Jaspers' proposal, which no one in Israel even bothered to discuss, would, in this form, presumably have been impracticable from a purely technical point of view. The question of a court's jurisdiction must be decided before the trial begins; and once a court has been declared competent, it must also pass judgment. However, these purely formalistic objections could easily have been met if Jaspers had called not upon the court, but rather upon the state of Israel to waive its right to carry out the sentence once it had been handed down, in view of the unprecedented nature of the court's findings. Israel might then have had recourse to the United Nations and demonstrated, with all the evidence at hand, that the need for an international criminal court was imperative, in view of these new crimes committed against mankind as a whole. It would then have been in Israel's power to make trouble, to 'create a wholesome disturbance', by asking again and again just what it should do with this man whom it was holding prisoner; constant repetition would have impressed on worldwide public opinion the need for a permanent international criminal court. Only by creating, in this way, an 'embarrassing situation' of concern to the representatives of all nations would it be possible to prevent 'mankind from setting its mind at ease' and 'massacre of the Jews ... from becoming a model for crimes to come, perhaps the small-scale and quite paltry example of future genocide'. The very monstrousness of the events is 'minimized' before a tribunal that represents one nation only.

This argument in favour of an international tribunal was unfortunately confused with other proposals based on different and considerably less weighty considerations. Many friends of Israel, both Jews and non-Jews feared that the trial would harm Israel's prestige and give rise to a reaction against Jews the world over. It was thought that Jews did not have the right to appear as judges in their own case, but could act only as accusers; Israel should therefore hold Eichmann prisoner until a special tribunal could be created by the United Nations to judge him. Quite apart from the fact that Israel, in the proceedings against Eichmann, was doing no more than what all the countries which had been occupied by Germany had long since done, and that justice was at stake here, not the prestige of Israel or of the Jewish people, all these proposals had one flaw in common: they could too easily be countered by Israel. They were indeed quite unrealistic in view of the fact that the

UN General Assembly had 'twice rejected proposals to consider the establishment of a permanent international criminal court' (*ADL Bulletin*). But another, more practical proposition, which usually is not mentioned precisely because it *was* feasible, was made by Dr Nahum Goldmann, president of the World Jewish Congress. Goldmann called upon Ben-Gurion to set up an international court in Jerusalem, with judges from each of the countries that had suffered under Nazi occupation. This would not have been enough; it would have been only an enlargement of the Successor trials, and the chief impairment of justice, that it was being rendered in the court of the victors, would not have been cured. But it would have been a practical step in the right direction.

Israel, as may be remembered, reacted against all these proposals with great violence. And while it is true, as has been pointed out by Yosal Rogat (in *The Eichmann Trial and the Rule of Law*, published by the Center for the Study of Democratic Institutions, Santa Barbara, California, 1962), that Ben-Gurion always 'seemed to misunderstand completely when asked, "Why should he not be tried before an international court?"' it is also true that those who asked the question did not understand that for Israel the only unprecedented feature of the trial was that, for the first time (since the year 70, when Jerusalem was destroyed by the Romans), Jews were able to sit in judgment on crimes committed against their own people, that, for the first time, they did not need to appeal to others for protection and justice, or fall back upon the compromised phraseology of the rights of man – rights which, as no one knew better than they, were claimed only by people who were too weak to defend their 'rights of Englishmen' and to enforce their own laws. (The very fact that Israel had her own law under which such a trial could be held had been called, long before the Eichmann trial, an expression of 'a revolutionary transformation that has taken place in the political position of the Jewish people' – by Mr Rosen on the occasion of the First Reading of the Law of 1950 in the Knesset.) It was against the background of these very vivid experiences and aspirations that Ben-Gurion said: 'Israel does not need the protection of an International Court.'

Moreover, the argument that the crime against the Jewish people was first of all a crime against mankind, upon which the valid proposals for an international tribunal rested, stood in flagrant contradiction to the law under which Eichmann was tried. Hence, those who proposed that Israel give up her prisoner should have gone one step further and declared: The Nazis and Nazi Collaborators (Punishment) Law of 1950 is wrong, it is in contradiction to what actually happened, it does not cover the facts. And this would indeed have been quite true. For just as a murderer is prosecuted because he has violated the law of the community, and not because he has deprived the Smith family of its husband, father, and breadwinner, so these modern, state-employed mass murderers must be prosecuted because they violated the order of mankind, and not because they killed millions of people. Nothing is more pernicious to an understanding of these new crimes, or stands more in the way of the emergence of an international penal code that could take care of them, than the common illusion that the crime of murder and the crime of genocide are essentially the same, and that the latter therefore is 'no new crime properly speaking'. The point of the latter is that an altogether different order is broken and an altogether different community is violated. And, indeed, it was because Ben-Gurion knew quite well that the whole discussion actually concerned the validity of the Israeli law that he finally reacted nastily, and not just with violence, against the critics of Israeli procedures: Whatever these 'so-called experts' had to say, their arguments were 'sophisms', inspired either by anti-Semitism, or, in the case of Jews, by inferiority complexes. 'Let the world understand: We shall not give up our prisoner.'

It is only fair to say that this was by no means the tone in which the trial was conducted in Jerusalem. But I think it is safe to predict that this last of the Successor trials will no more, and perhaps even less than its predecessors, serve as a valid precedent for future trials of such crimes. This might be of little import in view of the fact that its main purpose – to prosecute and to defend, to judge and to punish Adolf Eichmann – was achieved, if it were not for the rather uncomfortable but hardly deniable possibility that similar crimes may be committed in the future. The reasons for this sinister potentiality are general as well as particular. It is in the very nature of things human that every act that has once made its appearance and has been recorded in the history of mankind stays with mankind as a potentiality long after its actuality has become a thing of the past. No punishment has ever possessed enough power of deterrence to prevent the commission of crimes. On the contrary, whatever the punishment, once a specific crime has appeared for the first time, its reappearance is more likely than its initial emergence could ever have been. The particular reasons that speak for the possibility of a repetition of the crimes committed by the Nazis are even more plausible. The frightening coincidence of the modern population explosion with the discovery of technical devices that, through automation, will make large sections of the population 'superfluous' even in terms of labour, and that, through nuclear energy, make it possible to deal with this twofold threat by the use of instruments beside which Hitler's gassing installations look like an evil child's fumbling toys, should be enough to make us tremble.

It is essentially for this reason: that the unprecedented, once it has appeared, may become a precedent for the future, that all trials touching upon 'crimes against humanity' must be judged according to a standard that is today still an 'ideal'. If genocide is an actual possibility of the future, then no people on earth – least of all, of course, the Jewish people, in Israel or elsewhere – can feel reasonably sure of its continued existence without the help and the protection of international law. Success or failure in dealing with the hitherto unprecedented can lie only in the extent to which this dealing may serve as a valid precedent on the road to international penal law. And this demand, addressed to the judges in such trials, does not overshoot the mark and ask for more than can reasonably be expected. International law, Justice Jackson pointed out at Nuremberg, 'is an outgrowth of treaties and agreements between nations and of accepted customs. Yet every custom has its origin in some single act . . . Our own day has the right to institute customs and to conclude agreements that will themselves become sources of a newer and strengthened international law.' What Justice Jackson failed to point out is that, in consequence of this yet unfinished nature of international law, it has become the task of ordinary trial judges to render justice without the help of, or beyond the limitation set upon them through, positive, posited laws. For the judge, this may be a predicament, and he is only too likely to protest that the 'single act' demanded of him is not his to perform but is the business of the legislator.

And, indeed, before we come to any conclusion about the success or failure of the Jerusalem court, we must stress the judges' firm belief that they had no right to become legislators, that they had to conduct their business within the limits of Israeli law, on the one side, and of accepted legal opinion, on the other. It must be admitted furthermore that their failures were neither in kind nor in degree greater than the failures of the Nuremberg Trials or the Successor trials in other European countries. On the contrary, part of the failure of the Jerusalem court was due to its all too eager adherence to the Nuremberg precedent wherever possible.

In sum, the failure of the Jerusalem court consisted in its not coming to grips with three fundamental issues, all of which have been sufficiently well known and widely discussed since the establishment of the Nuremberg Tribunal: the problem of impaired justice in the court of the victors; a valid definition of the 'crime against humanity'; and a clear recognition of the new criminal who commits this crime.

As to the first of these, justice was more seriously impaired in Jerusalem than it was at Nuremberg, because the court did not admit witnesses for the defence. In terms of the traditional requirements for fair and due process of law, this was the most serious flaw in the Jerusalem proceedings. Moreover, while judgment in the court of the victors was perhaps inevitable at the close of the war (to Justice Jackson's argument in Nuremberg: 'Either the victors must judge the vanquished or we must leave the defeated to judge themselves,' should be added the understandable feeling on the part of the Allies that they 'who had risked everything could not admit neutrals' (Vabres)), it was not the same sixteen years later, and under circumstances in which the argument against the admission of neutral countries did not make sense.

As to the second issue, the findings of the Jerusalem court were incomparably better than those at Nuremberg. I have mentioned before the Nuremberg Charter's definition of 'crimes against humanity' as 'inhuman acts', which were translated into German as *Verbrechen gegen die Menschlichkeit* – as though the Nazis had simply been lacking in human kindness, certainly the understatement of the century. To be sure, had the conduct of the Jerusalem trial depended entirely upon the prosecution, the basic misunderstanding would have been even worse than at Nuremberg. But the judgment refused to let the basic character of the crime be swallowed up in a flood of atrocities, and it did not fall into the trap of equating this crime with ordinary war crimes. What had been mentioned at Nuremberg only occasionally and, as it were, marginally – that 'the evidence shows that . . . the mass murders and cruelties were not committed solely for the purpose of stamping out opposition' but were 'part of a plan to get rid of whole native populations' – was in the centre of the Jerusalem proceedings, for the obvious reason that Eichmann stood accused of a crime against the Jewish people, a crime that could not be explained by any utilitarian purpose; Jews had been murdered all over Europe, not only in the East, and their annihilation was not due to any desire to gain territory that 'could be used for colonization by Germans'. It was the great advantage of a trial centred on the crime against the Jewish people that not only did the difference between war crimes, such as shooting of partisans and killing of hostages, and 'inhuman acts', such as 'expulsion and annihilation' of native populations to permit colonization by an invader, emerge with sufficient clarity to become part of a future international penal code, but also that the difference between 'inhuman acts' (which were undertaken for some known, though criminal, purpose, such as expansion through colonization) and the 'crime against humanity', whose intent and purpose were unprecedented, was clarified. At no point, however, either in the proceedings or in the judgment, did the Jerusalem trial ever mention even the possibility that extermination of whole ethnic groups – the Jews, or the Poles, or the Gypsies – might be more than a crime against the Jewish or the Polish or the Gypsy people, that the international order, and mankind in its entirety, might have been grievously hurt and endangered.

Closely connected with this failure was the conspicuous helplessness the judges experienced when they were confronted with the task they could least escape, the task of understanding the criminal whom they had come to judge. Clearly, it was not enough that they did not follow the prosecution in its obviously mistaken description of the accused as a 'perverted sadist', nor would it have been enough if they had gone one step further and shown the inconsistency of the case for the prosecution, in which Mr Hausner wanted to try the most abnormal monster the world had ever seen and, at the same time, try in him 'many like him', even the 'whole Nazi movement and anti-Semitism at large'. They knew, of course, that it would have been very comforting indeed to believe that Eichmann was a monster, even though if he had been Israel's case against him would have collapsed or, at the very least, lost all interest. Surely, one can hardly call upon the whole world and gather correspondents from the four corners of the earth in order to display Bluebeard in the dock. The trouble with Eichmann was precisely that so many were like him, and that the many were neither perverted nor sadistic, that they were, and still are, terribly and terrifyingly normal. From the viewpoint of our legal institutions and of our moral standards of judgment, this normality was much more terrifying than all the atrocities put together, for it implied – as had been said at Nuremberg over and over again by the defendants and their counsels – that this new type of criminal, who is in actual fact *hostis generis humani*, commits his crimes under circumstances that make it well-nigh impossible for him to know or to feel that he is doing wrong. In this respect, the evidence in the Eichmann case was even more convincing than the evidence presented in the trial of the major war criminals, whose pleas of a clear conscience could be dismissed more easily because they combined with the argument of obedience to 'superior orders' various boasts about occasional disobedience. But although the bad faith of the defendants was manifest, the only ground on which guilty conscience could actually be proved was the fact that the Nazis, and especially the criminal organizations to which Eichmann belonged, had been so very busy destroying the evidence of their crimes during the last months of the war. And this ground was rather shaky. It proved no more than recognition that the law of mass murder, because of its novelty, was not yet accepted by other nations; or, in the language of the Nazis, that they had lost their fight to 'liberate' mankind from the 'rule of subhumans', especially from the domination of the Elders of Zion; or, in ordinary language, it proved no more than the admission of defeat. Would any one of them have suffered from a guilty conscience if they had won?

Foremost among the larger issues at stake in the Eichmann trial was the assumption current in all modern legal systems that intent to do wrong is necessary for the commission of a crime. On nothing, perhaps, has civilized jurisprudence prided itself more than on this taking into account of the subjective factor. Where this intent is absent, where, for whatever reasons, even reasons of moral insanity, the ability to distinguish between right and wrong is impaired, we feel no crime has been committed. We refuse, and consider as barbaric, the propositions 'that a great crime offends nature, so that the very earth cries out for vengeance; that evil violates a natural harmony which only retribution can restore; that a wronged collectivity owes a duty to the moral order to punish the criminal' (Yosal Rogat). And yet I think it is undeniable that it was precisely on the ground of these long-forgotten propositions that Eichmann was brought to justice to begin with, and that they were, in fact, the supreme justification for the death penalty. Because he had been implicated and had played a central role in an enterprise whose open purpose was to eliminate forever certain 'races' from the surface of the earth, he had to be eliminated. And if it is true that 'justice must not only be done but must be seen to be done,' then the justice of what was done in Jerusalem would have emerged to be seen by all if the judges had dared to address their defendant in something like the following terms:

'You admitted that the crime committed against the Jewish people during the war was the greatest crime in recorded history, and you admitted your role in it. But you said you had never acted from base motives, that you had never had any inclination to kill anybody, that you had never hated Jews, and still that you could not have acted otherwise and that you did not feel guilty. We find this difficult, though not altogether impossible, to believe; there is some, though not very much, evidence against you in this matter of motivation and conscience that could be proved beyond reasonable doubt.

You also said that your role in the Final Solution was an accident and that almost anybody could have taken your place, so that potentially almost all Germans are equally guilty. What you meant to say was that where all, or almost all, are guilty, nobody is. This is an indeed quite common conclusion, but one we are not willing to grant you. And if you don't understand our objection, we would recommend to your attention the story of Sodom and Gomorrah, two neighbouring cities in the Bible, which were destroyed by fire from Heaven because all the people in them had become equally guilty. This, incidentally, has nothing to do with the newfangled notion of 'collective guilt', according to which people supposedly are guilty of, or feel guilty about, things done in their name but not by them – things in which they did not participate and from which they did not profit. In other words, guilt and innocence before the law are of an objective nature, and even if eighty million Germans had done as you did, this would not have been an excuse for you.

'Luckily, we don't have to go that far. You yourself claimed not the actuality but only the potentiality of equal guilt on the part of all who lived in a state whose main political purpose had become the commission of unheard-of crimes. And no matter through what accidents of exterior or interior circumstances you were pushed onto the road of becoming a criminal, there is an abyss between the actuality of what you did and the potentiality of what others might have done. We are concerned here only with what you did, and not with the possible non-criminal nature of your inner life and of your motives or with the criminal potentialities of those around you. You told your story in terms of a hard-luck story, and, knowing the circumstances, we are, up to a point, willing to grant you that under more favourable circumstances it is highly unlikely that you would ever have come before us or before any other criminal court. Let us assume, for the sake of argument, that it was nothing more than misfortune that made you a willing instrument in the organization of mass murder; there still remains the fact that you have carried out, and therefore actively supported, a policy of mass murder. For politics is not like the nursery; in politics obedience and support are the same. And just as you supported and carried out a policy of not wanting to share the earth with the Jewish people and the people of a number of other nations – as though you and your superiors had any right to determine who should and who should not inhabit the world – we find that no one, that is, no member of the human race, can be expected to want to share the earth with you. This is the reason, and the only reason, you must hang.'

Postscript

[...] Even before its publication, this book became both the centre of a controversy and the object of an organized campaign. It is only natural that the campaign, conducted with all the well-known means of image-making and opinion-manipulation, got much more attention than the controversy, so that the latter was somehow swallowed up by and drowned in the artificial noise of the former. This became especially clear when a strange mixture of the two, in almost identical phraseology – as though the pieces written against the book (and more frequently against its author) came 'out of a mimeographing machine' (Mary McCarthy) – was carried from America to England and then to Europe, where the book was not yet even available. And this was possible because the clamour centred on the 'image' of a book which was never written, and touched upon subjects that often had not only not been mentioned by me but had never occurred to me before.

The debate – if that is what it was – was by no means devoid of interest. Manipulations of opinion, insofar as they are inspired by well-defined interests, have limited goals; their effect, however, if they happen to touch upon an issue of authentic concern, is no longer subject to their control and may easily produce consequences they never foresaw or intended. It now appeared that the era of the Hitler regime, with its gigantic, unprecedented crimes, constituted an 'unmastered past' not only for the German people or for the Jews all over the world, but for the rest of the world, which had not forgotten this great catastrophe in the heart of Europe either, and had also been unable to come to terms with it. Moreover – and this was perhaps even less expected – general moral questions, with all their intricacies and modern complexities, which I would never have suspected would haunt men's minds today and weigh heavily on their hearts, stood suddenly in the foreground of public concern.

The controversy began by calling attention to the conduct of the Jewish people during the years of the Final Solution, thus following up the question, first raised by the Israeli prosecutor, of whether the Jews could or should have defended themselves. I had dismissed that question as silly and cruel, since it testified to a fatal ignorance of the conditions at the time. It has now been discussed to exhaustion, and the most amazing conclusions have been drawn. The well-known historico-sociological construct of a 'ghetto mentality' (which in Israel has taken its place in history textbooks and in this country has been espoused chiefly by the psychologist Bruno Bettelheim – against the furious protest of official American Judaism) has been repeatedly dragged in to explain behaviour which was not at all confined to the Jewish people and which therefore cannot be explained by specifically Jewish factors. The suggestions proliferated until someone who evidently found the whole discussion too dull had the brilliant idea of evoking Freudian theories and attributing to the whole Jewish people a 'death wish' – unconscious, of course. This was the unexpected conclusion certain reviewers chose to draw from the 'image' of a book, created by certain interest groups, in which I allegedly had claimed that the Jews had murdered themselves. And why had I told such a monstrously implausible lie? Out of 'self-hatred', of course.

Since the role of the Jewish leadership had come up at the trial, and since I had reported and commented on it, it was inevitable that it too should be discussed. This, in my opinion, is a serious question, but the debate has contributed little to its clarification. As can be seen from the recent trial in Israel at which a certain Hirsch Birnblat, a former chief of the Jewish police in a Polish town and now a conductor at the Israeli Opera first was sentenced by a district court to five years' imprisonment, and then was exonerated by the Supreme Court in Jerusalem, whose unanimous opinion indirectly exonerated the Jewish Councils in general, the Jewish Establishment is bitterly divided on this issue. In the debate, however, the most vocal participants were those who either identified the Jewish people with its leadership – in striking contrast to the clear distinction made in almost all the reports of survivors, which may be summed up in the words of a former inmate of Theresienstadt: 'The Jewish people as a whole behaved magnificently. Only the leadership failed' – or justified the Jewish functionaries by citing all the commendable services they had rendered before the war, and above all before the era of the Final Solution, as though there were no difference between helping Jews to emigrate and helping the Nazis to deport them.

While these issues had indeed some connection with this book, although they were inflated out of all proportion, there were others which had no relation to it whatsoever. There was, for instance, a hot discussion of the German resistance movement from the beginning of the Hitler regime on, which I naturally did not discuss, since the question of Eichmann's conscience, and that of the situation around him, relates only to the period of the war and the Final Solution. But there were more fantastic items. Quite a number of people began to debate the question of whether the victims of persecution may not always be 'uglier' than their murderers; or whether anyone who was not present is entitled 'to sit in judgment' over the past; or whether the defendant or the victim holds the centre of the stage in a trial. On the latter point, some went so far as to assert not only that I was wrong in being interested in what kind of person Eichmann was, but that he should not have been allowed to speak at all – that is, presumably, that the trial should have been conducted without any defence.

As is frequently the case in discussions that are conducted with a great show of emotion, the down-to-earth interests of certain groups, whose excitement is entirely concerned with factual matters and who therefore try to distort the facts, become quickly and inextricably involved with the untrammelled inspirations of intellectuals who, on the contrary, are not in the least interested in facts but treat them merely as a springboard for 'ideas'. But even in these sham battles, there could often be detected a certain seriousness, a degree of authentic concern, and this even in the contributions by people who boasted that they had not read the book and promised that they never would read it.

Compared with these debates, which wandered so far afield, the book itself dealt with a sadly limited subject. The report of a trial can discuss only the matters which were treated in the course of the trial, or which in the interests of justice should have been treated. If the general situation of a country in which the trial takes place happens to be important to the conduct of the trial, it too must be taken into account. This book, then, does not deal with the history of the greatest disaster that ever befell the Jewish people, nor is it an account of totalitarianism, or a history of the German people in the time of the Third Reich, nor is it, finally and least of all, a theoretical treatise on the nature of evil. The focus of every trial is upon the person of the defendant, a man of flesh and blood with an individual history, with an always unique set of qualities, peculiarities, behaviour patterns, and circumstances. All the things that go beyond that, such as the history of the Jewish people in the dispersion, and of anti-Semitism, or the conduct of the German people and other peoples, or the ideologies of the time and the governmental apparatus of the Third Reich, affect the trial only insofar as they form the background and the conditions under which the defendant committed his acts. All the things that the defendant did not come into contact with, or that did not influence him, must be omitted from the proceedings of the trial and consequently from the report on it.

It may be argued that all the general questions we involuntarily raise as soon as we begin to speak of these matters – why did it have to be the Germans? why did it have to be the Jews? what is the nature of totalitarian rule? – are far more important than the question of the kind of crime for which a man is being tried, and the nature of the defendant upon whom justice must be pronounced; more important, too, than the question of how well our present system of justice is capable of dealing with this special type of crime and criminal it has had repeatedly to cope with since the Second World War. It can be held that the issue is no longer a particular human being, a single distinct individual in the dock, but rather the

German people in general, or anti-Semitism in all its forms, or the whole of modern history, or the nature of man and original sin – so that ultimately the entire human race sits invisibly beside the defendant in the dock. All this has often been argued, and especially by those who will not rest until they have discovered an 'Eichmann in every one of us'. If the defendant is taken as a symbol and the trial as a pretext to bring up matters which are apparently more interesting than the guilt or innocence of one person, then consistency demands that we bow to the assertion made by Eichmann and his lawyer: that he was brought to book because a scapegoat was needed, not only for the German Federal Republic, but also for the events as a whole and for what made them possible – that is, for anti-Semitism and totalitarian government as well as for the human race and original sin.

I need scarcely say that I would never have gone to Jerusalem if I had shared these views. I held and hold the opinion that this trial had to take place in the interests of justice and nothing else. I also think the judges were quite right when they stressed in their verdict that 'the State of Israel was established and recognized as the State of the Jews,' and therefore had jurisdiction over a crime committed against the Jewish people; and in view of the current confusion in legal circles about the meaning and usefulness of punishment, I was glad that the judgment quoted Grotius, who, for his part, citing an older author, explained that punishment is necessary 'to defend the honour or the authority of him who was hurt by the offence so that the failure to punish may not cause his degradation'.

There is of course no doubt that the defendant and the nature of his acts as well as the trial itself raise problems of a general nature which go far beyond the matters considered in Jerusalem. I have attempted to go into some of these problems in the Epilogue, which ceases to be simple reporting. I would not have been surprised if people had found my treatment inadequate, and I would have welcomed a discussion of the general significance of the entire body of facts, which could have been all the more meaningful the more directly it referred to the concrete events. I also can well imagine that an authentic controversy might have arisen over the subtitle of the book; for when I speak of the banality of evil, I do so only on the strictly factual level, pointing to a phenomenon which stared one in the face at the trial. Eichmann was not Iago and not Macbeth, and nothing would have been farther from his mind than to determine with Richard III 'to prove a villain'. Except for an extraordinary diligence in looking out for his personal advancement, he had no motives at all. And this diligence in itself was in no way criminal; he certainly would never have murdered his superior in order to inherit his post. He *merely*, to put the matter colloquially, *never realized what he was doing*. It was precisely this lack of imagination which enabled him to sit for months on end facing a German Jew who was conducting the police interrogation, pouring out his heart to the man and explaining again and again how it was that he reached only the rank of lieutenant colonel in the SS and that it had not been his fault that he was not promoted. In principle he knew quite well what it was all about, and in his final statement to the court he spoke of the 'revaluation of values prescribed by the [Nazi] government'. He was not stupid. It was sheer thoughtlessness – something by no means identical with stupidity – that predisposed him to become one of the greatest criminals of that period. And if this is 'banal' and even funny, if with the best will in the world one cannot extract any diabolical or demonic profundity from Eichmann, that is still far from calling it commonplace. It surely cannot be so common that a man facing death, and, moreover, standing beneath the gallows, should be able to think of nothing but what he has heard at funerals all his life, and that these 'lofty words' should completely becloud the reality of his own death. That such remoteness from reality and such thoughtlessness can wreak more havoc than all the evil instincts taken together which, perhaps, are inherent in man – that was, in fact, the lesson one could learn in Jerusalem. But it was a lesson, neither an explanation of the phenomenon nor a theory about it.

Seemingly more complicated, but in reality far simpler than examining the strange interdependence of thoughtlessness and evil, is the question of what kind of crime is actually involved here – a crime, moreover, which all agree is unprecedented. For the concept of genocide, introduced explicitly to cover a crime unknown before, although applicable up to a point is not fully adequate, for the simple reason that massacres of whole peoples are not unprecedented. They were the order of the day in antiquity, and the centuries of colonization and imperialism provide plenty of examples of more or less successful attempts of that sort. The expression 'administrative massacres' seems better to fill the bill. The term arose in connection with British imperialism; the English deliberately rejected such procedures as a means of maintaining their rule over India. The phrase has the virtue of dispelling the prejudice that such monstrous acts can be committed only against a foreign nation or a different race. There is the well-known fact that Hitler began his mass murders by granting 'mercy deaths' to the 'incurably ill', and that he intended to wind up his extermination programme by doing away with 'genetically damaged' Germans (heart and lung patients). But quite aside from that, it is apparent that this sort of killing can be directed against any given group, that is, that the principle of selection is dependent only upon circumstantial factors. It is quite conceivable that in the automated economy of a not-too-distant future men may be tempted to exterminate all those whose intelligence quotient is below a certain level.

In Jerusalem this matter was inadequately discussed because it is actually very difficult to grasp juridically. We heard the protestations of the defence that Eichmann was after all only a 'tiny cog' in the machinery of the Final Solution, and of the prosecution, which believed it had discovered in Eichmann the actual motor. I myself attributed no more importance to both theories than did the Jerusalem court, since the whole cog theory is legally pointless and therefore it does not matter at all what order of magnitude is assigned to the 'cog' named Eichmann. In its judgment the court naturally conceded that such a crime could be committed only by a giant bureaucracy using the resources of government. But insofar as it remains a crime – and that, of course, is the premise for a trial – all the cogs in the machinery, no matter how insignificant, are in court forthwith transformed back into perpetrators, that is to say, into human beings. If the defendant excuses himself on the ground that he acted not as a man but as a mere functionary whose functions could just as easily have been carried out by anyone else, it is as if a criminal pointed to the statistics on crime – which set forth that so-and-so many crimes per day are committed in such-and-such a place – and declared that he only did what was statistically expected, that it was mere accident that he did it and not somebody else, since after all somebody had to do it.

Of course it is important to the political and social sciences that the essence of totalitarian government, and perhaps the nature of every bureaucracy, is to make functionaries and mere cogs in the administrative machinery out of men, and thus to dehumanize them. And one can debate long and profitably on the rule of Nobody, which is what the political form known as bureaucracy truly is. Only one must realize clearly that the administration of justice can consider these factors only to the extent that they are circumstances of the crime – just as, in a case of theft, the economic plight of the thief is taken into account without excusing the theft, let alone wiping it off the slate. True, we have become very much accustomed by modern psychology and sociology, not to speak of modern bureaucracy, to explaining away the responsibility of the doer for his deed in terms of this or that kind of determinism. Whether such seemingly deeper explanations of human actions are right or wrong is debatable. But what is not debatable is that no judicial procedure would be possible on the basis of them, and that the administration of justice, measured by such theories, is an extremely unmodern, not to say outmoded, institution. When Hitler said that a day would come in Germany when it would be considered a 'disgrace' to be a jurist, he was speaking with utter consistency of his dream of a perfect bureaucracy.

As far as I can see, jurisprudence has at its disposal for treating this whole battery of questions only two categories, both of which, to my mind, are quite inadequate to deal with the matter. These are the concepts of 'acts of state' and of acts 'on superior orders'. At any rate, these are the only categories in terms of which such matters are discussed in this kind of trial, usually on the motion of the defendant. The theory of the act of state is based on the argument that one sovereign state may not sit in judgment upon another, *par in parem non habet jurisdictionem*. Practically speaking, this argument had already been disposed of at Nuremberg; it stood no chance from the start, since, if it were accepted, even Hitler, the only one who was really responsible in the full sense, could not have been brought to account – a state of affairs which would have violated the most elementary sense of justice. However, an argument that stands no chance on the practical plane has not necessarily been demolished on the theoretical one. The usual evasions – that Germany at the time of the Third Reich was dominated by a gang of criminals to whom sovereignty and party cannot very well be ascribed – were hardly useful. For on the one hand everyone knows that the analogy with a gang of criminals is applicable only to such a limited extent that it is not really applicable at all, and on the other hand these crimes undeniably took place within a 'legal' order. That, indeed, was their outstanding characteristic.

Perhaps we can approach somewhat closer to the matter if we realize that behind the concept of act of state stands the theory of *raison d'état*. According to that theory, the actions of the state, which is responsible for the life of the country and thus also for the laws obtaining in it, are not subject to the same rules as the acts of the citizens of the country. Just as the rule of law, although devised to eliminate violence and the war of all against all, always stands in need of the instruments of violence in order to assure its own existence, so a government may find itself compelled to commit actions that are generally regarded as crimes in order to assure its own survival and the survival of lawfulness. Wars are frequently justified on these grounds, but criminal acts of state do not occur only in the field of international relations, and the history of civilized nations knows many examples of them – from Napoleon's assassination of the Duc d'Enghien, to the murder of the Socialist leader Matteotti, for which Mussolini himself was presumably responsible.

Raison d'état appeals – rightly or wrongly, as the case may be – to *necessity*, and the state crimes committed in its name (which are fully criminal in terms of the dominant legal system of the country where they occur) are considered emergency measures, concessions made to the stringencies of *Realpolitik*, in order to preserve power and thus assure the continuance of the existing legal order as a whole. In a normal political and legal system, such crimes occur as an exception to the rule and are not subject to legal penalty (are *gerichtsfrei*, as German legal theory expresses it), because the existence of the state itself is at stake, and no outside political entity has the right to deny a state its existence or prescribe how it is to preserve it. However – as we may have learned from the history of Jewish policy in the Third Reich – in a state founded upon criminal principles, the situation is reversed. Then a non-criminal act (such as, for example, Himmler's order in the late summer of 1944 to halt the deportation of Jews) becomes a concession to necessity imposed by reality, in this case the impending defeat. Here the question arises: what is the nature of the sovereignty of such an entity? Has it not violated the parity (*par in parem non habet jurisdictionem*) which international law accords it? Does the '*par in parem*' signify no more than the paraphernalia of sovereignty? Or does it also imply a substantive equality or likeness? Can we apply the same principle that is applied to a governmental apparatus in which crime and violence are exceptions and borderline cases to a political order in which crime is legal and the rule?

Just how inadequate juristic concepts really are to deal with the criminal facts which were the subject matter of all these trials appears perhaps even more strikingly in the concept of acts performed on superior orders. The Jerusalem court countered the argument advanced by the defence with lengthy quotations from the penal and military lawbooks of civilized countries, particularly of

Germany; for under Hitler the pertinent articles had by no means been repealed. All of them agree on one point: manifestly criminal orders must not be obeyed. The court, moreover, referred to a case that came up in Israel several years ago: soldiers were brought to trial for having massacred the civilian inhabitants of an Arab village on the border shortly before the beginning of the Sinai campaign. The villagers had been found outside their houses during a military curfew of which, it appeared, they were unaware. Unfortunately, on closer examination the comparison appears to be defective on two accounts. First of all, we must again consider that the relationship of exception and rule, which is of prime importance for recognizing the criminality of an order executed by a subordinate, was reversed in the case of Eichmann's actions. Thus, on the basis of this argument one could actually defend Eichmann's failure to obey certain of Himmler's orders, or his obeying them with hesitancy: they were manifest exceptions to the prevailing rule. The judgment found this to be especially incriminating to the defendant, which was certainly very understandable but not very consistent. This can easily be seen from the pertinent findings of Israeli military courts, which were cited in support by the judges. They ran as follows: the order to be disobeyed must be 'manifestly unlawful'; unlawfulness 'should fly like a black flag above [it], as a warning reading, "Prohibited"'. In other words, the order, to be recognized by the soldier as 'manifestly unlawful', must violate by its unusualness the canons of the legal system to which he is accustomed. And Israeli jurisprudence in these matters coincides completely with that of other countries. No doubt in formulating these articles the legislators were thinking of cases in which an officer who suddenly goes mad, say, commands his subordinates to kill another officer. In any normal trial of such a case, it would at once become clear that the soldier was not being asked to consult the voice of conscience, or a 'feeling of lawfulness that lies deep within every human conscience, also of those who are not conversant with books of law . . . provided the eye is not blind and the heart is not stony and corrupt'. Rather, the soldier would be expected to be able to distinguish between a rule and a striking exception to the rule. The German military code, at any rate, explicitly states that conscience is not enough. Paragraph 48 reads: 'Punishability of an action or omission is not excluded on the ground that the person considered his behaviour required by his conscience or the prescripts of his religion.' A striking feature of the Israeli court's line of argument is that the concept of a sense of justice grounded in the depths of every man is presented solely as a substitute for familiarity with the law. Its plausibility rests on the assumption that the law expresses only what every man's conscience would tell him anyhow.

If we are to apply this whole reasoning to the Eichmann case in a meaningful way, we are forced to conclude that Eichmann acted fully within the framework of the kind of judgment required of him: he acted in accordance with the rule, examined the order issued to him for its 'manifest' legality, namely regularity; he did not have to fall back upon his 'conscience', since he was not one of those who were unfamiliar with the laws of his country. The exact opposite was the case.

The second account on which the argument based on comparison proved to be defective concerns the practice of the courts of admitting the plea of 'superior orders' as important extenuating circumstances, and this practice was mentioned explicitly by the judgment. The judgment cited the case I have mentioned above, that of the massacre of the Arab inhabitants at Kfar Kassem, as proof that Israeli jurisdiction does not clear a defendant of responsibility for the 'superior orders' he received. And it is true, the Israeli soldiers were indicted for murder, but 'superior orders' constituted so weighty an argument for mitigating circumstances that they were sentenced to relatively short prison terms. To be sure, this case concerned an isolated act, not – as in Eichmann's case – an activity extending over years, in which crime followed crime. Still, it was undeniable that he had always acted upon 'superior orders', and if the provisions of ordinary Israeli law had been applied to him, it would have been difficult indeed to impose the maximum penalty upon him. The truth of the matter is that Israeli law, in theory and practice, like the jurisdiction of other countries cannot but admit that the fact of 'superior orders', even when their unlawfulness is 'manifest', can severely disturb the normal working of a man's conscience.

This is only one example among many to demonstrate the inadequacy of the prevailing legal system and of current juridical concepts to deal with the facts of administrative massacres organized by the state apparatus. If we look more closely into the matter we will observe without much difficulty that the judges in all these trials really passed judgment solely on the basis of the monstrous deeds. In other words, they judged freely, as it were, and did not really lean on the standards and legal precedents with which they more or less convincingly sought to justify their decisions. That was already evident in Nuremberg, where the judges on the one hand declared that the 'crime against peace' was the gravest of all the crimes they had to deal with, since it included all the other crimes, but on the other hand actually imposed the death penalty only on those defendants who had participated in the new crime of administrative massacre – supposedly a less grave offence than conspiracy against peace. It would indeed be tempting to pursue these and similar inconsistencies in a field so obsessed with consistency as jurisprudence. But of course that cannot be done here.

There remains, however, one fundamental problem, which was implicitly present in all these postwar trials and which must be mentioned here because it touches upon one of the central moral questions of all time, namely upon the nature and function of human judgment. What we have demanded in these trials, where the defendants had committed 'legal' crimes, is that human beings be capable of telling right from wrong even when all they have to guide them is their own judgment, which, moreover, happens to be completely at odds with what they must regard as the unanimous opinion of all those around them. And this question is all the more serious as we know that the few who were 'arrogant' enough to trust only their own judgment were by no means identical with those persons who continued to abide by old values, or who were guided by a religious belief. Since the whole of respectable society had in one way or another succumbed to Hitler, the moral maxims which determine social behaviour and the religious commandments – 'Thou shalt not kill!' – which guide conscience had virtually vanished. Those few who were still able to tell right from wrong went really only by their own judgments, and they did so freely; there were no rules to be abided by, under which the particular cases with which they were confronted could be subsumed. They had to decide each instance as it arose, because no rules existed for the unprecedented.

How troubled men of our time are by this question of judgment (or, as is often said, by people who dare 'sit in judgment') has emerged in the controversy over the present book, as well as the in many respects similar controversy over Hochhuth's *The Deputy*. What has come to light is neither nihilism nor cynicism, as one might have expected, but a quite extraordinary confusion over elementary questions of morality – as if an instinct in such matters were truly the last thing to be taken for granted in our time. The many curious notes that have been struck in the course of these disputes seem particularly revealing. Thus, some American literati have professed their naïve belief that temptation and coercion are really the same thing, that no one can be asked to resist temptation. (If someone puts a pistol to your heart and orders you to shoot your best friend, then you simply *must* shoot him. Or, as it was argued – some years ago in connection with the quiz programme scandal in which a university teacher had hoaxed the public – when so much money is at stake, who could possibly resist?) The argument that we cannot judge if we were not present and involved ourselves seems to convince everyone everywhere, although it seems obvious that if it were true, neither the administration of justice nor the writing of history would ever be possible. In contrast to these confusions, the reproach of self-righteousness raised against those who do judge is age-old; but that does not make it any the more valid. Even the judge who condemns a murderer can still say when he goes home: 'And there, but for the grace of God, go I.' All German Jews unanimously have condemned the wave of co-ordination which passed over the German people in 1933 and from one day to the next turned the Jews into pariahs. Is it conceivable that none of them ever asked himself how many of his own group would have done just the same if only they had been allowed to? But is their condemnation today any the less correct for that reason?

The reflection that you yourself might have done wrong under the same circumstances may kindle a spirit of forgiveness, but those who today refer to Christian charity seem strangely confused on this issue too. Thus we can read in the postwar statement of the *Evangelische Kirche in Deutschland*, the Protestant church, as follows: 'We aver that before the God of Mercy we share in the guilt for the outrage committed against the Jews by our own people through omission and silence.'* It seems to me that a Christian is guilty before the God of *Mercy* if he repays evil with evil, hence that the churches would have sinned against mercy if millions of Jews had been killed as punishment for some evil they committed. But if the churches shared in the guilt for an outrage pure and simple, as they themselves attest, then the matter must still be considered to fall within the purview of the God of *Justice*.

This slip of the tongue, as it were, is no accident. Justice, but not mercy, is a matter of judgment, and about nothing does public opinion everywhere seem to be in happier agreement than that no one has the right to judge somebody else. What public opinion permits us to judge and even to condemn are trends, or whole groups of people – the larger the better – in short, something so general that distinctions can no longer be made, names no longer be named. Needless to add, this taboo applies doubly when the deeds or words of famous people or men in high position are being questioned. This is currently expressed in high-flown assertions that it is 'superficial' to insist on details and to mention individuals, whereas it is the sign of sophistication to speak in generalities according to which all cats are grey and we are all equally guilty. Thus the charge Hochhuth has raised against a single Pope – one man, easily identi-fiable, with a name of his own – was immediately

* Quoted from the minister Aurel v. Jüchen in an anthology of critical reviews of Hochhuth's play – *Summa Iniuria*, Rowohl, Verlag, p. 195.

countered with an indictment of all Christianity. The charge against Christianity in general, with its two thousand years of history, cannot be proved, and if it could be proved, it would be horrible. No one seems to mind this so long as no *person* is involved, and it is quite safe to go one step further and to maintain: 'Undoubtedly there is reason for grave accusations, but the defendant is *mankind* as a whole.' (Thus Robert Weltsch in *Summa Iniuria*, quoted above, italics added.)

Another such escape from the area of ascertainable facts and personal responsibility are the countless theories, based on non-specific, abstract, hypothetical assumptions – from the *Zeitgeist* down to the Oedipus complex – which are so general that they explain and justify every event and every deed: no alternative to what actually happened is even considered and no person could have acted differently from the way he did act. Among the constructs that 'explain' everything by obscuring all details, we find such notions as a 'ghetto mentality' among European Jews; or the collective guilt of the German people, derived from an *ad hoc* interpretation of their history; or the equally absurd assertion of a kind of collective innocence of the Jewish people. All these clichés have in common that they make judgment superfluous and that to utter them is devoid of all risk. And although we can understand the reluctance of those immediately affected by the disaster – Germans and Jews – to examine too closely the conduct of groups and persons that seemed to be or should have been unimpaired by the totality of the moral collapse – that is, the conduct of the Christian churches, the Jewish leadership, the men of the anti-Hitler conspiracy of July 20, 1944 – this understandable disinclination is insufficient to explain the reluctance evident everywhere to make judgments in terms of individual moral responsibility.

Many people today would agree that there is no such thing as collective guilt or, for that matter, collective innocence, and that if there were, no one person could ever be guilty or innocent. This, of course, is not to deny that there is such a thing as *political* responsibility which, however, exists quite apart from what the individual member of the group has done and therefore can neither be judged in moral terms nor be brought before a criminal court. Every government assumes political responsibility for the deeds and misdeeds of its predecessor and every nation for the deeds and misdeeds of the past. When Napoleon, seizing power in France after the Revolution, said: I shall assume the responsibility for everything France ever did from Saint Louis to the Committee of Public Safety, he was only stating somewhat emphatically one of the basic facts of all political life. It means hardly more, generally speaking, than that every generation, by virtue of being born into a historical continuum, is burdened by the sins of the fathers as it is blessed with the deeds of the ancestors. But this kind of responsibility is not what we are talking about here; it is not personal, and only in a metaphorical sense can one say he *feels* guilty for what not he but his father or his people have done. (Morally speaking, it is hardly less wrong to feel guilty without having done something specific than it is to feel free of all guilt if one is actually guilty of something.) It is quite conceivable that certain political

responsibilities among nations might some day be adjudi-
cated in an international court; what is inconceivable is
that such a court would be a criminal tribunal which
pronounces on the guilt or innocence of individuals.

And the question of individual guilt or innocence, the
act of meting out justice to both the defendant and the
victim, are the only things at stake in a criminal court.
The Eichmann trial was no exception, even though the
court here was confronted with a crime it could not find
in the lawbooks and with a criminal whose like was
unknown in any court, at least prior to the Nuremberg
Trials. The present report deals with nothing but the
extent to which the court in Jerusalem succeeded in
fulfilling the demands of justice.

FOR THE BEST IN PAPERBACKS, LOOK FOR THE

In every corner of the world, on every subject under the sun, Penguin represents quality and variety—the very best in publishing today.

For complete information about books available from Penguin—including Penguin Classics, Penguin Compass, and Puffins—and how to order them, write to us at the appropriate address below. Please note that for copyright reasons the selection of books varies from country to country.

In the United States: Please write to *Penguin Group (USA), P.O. Box 12289 Dept. B, Newark, New Jersey 07101-5289* or call 1-800-788-6262.

In the United Kingdom: Please write to *Dept. EP, Penguin Books Ltd, Bath Road, Harmondsworth, West Drayton, Middlesex UB7 0DA.*

In Canada: Please write to *Penguin Books Canada Ltd, 90 Eglinton Avenue East, Suite 700, Toronto, Ontario M4P 2Y3.*

In Australia: Please write to *Penguin Books Australia Ltd, P.O. Box 257, Ringwood, Victoria 3134.*

In New Zealand: Please write to *Penguin Books (NZ) Ltd, Private Bag 102902, North Shore Mail Centre, Auckland 10.*

In India: Please write to *Penguin Books India Pvt Ltd, 11 Panchsheel Shopping Centre, Panchsheel Park, New Delhi 110 017.*

In the Netherlands: Please write to *Penguin Books Netherlands bv, Postbus 3507, NL-1001 AH Amsterdam.*

In Germany: Please write to *Penguin Books Deutschland GmbH, Metzlerstrasse 26, 60594 Frankfurt am Main.*

In Spain: Please write to *Penguin Books S. A., Bravo Murillo 19, 1° B, 28015 Madrid.*

In Italy: Please write to *Penguin Italia s.r.l., Via Benedetto Croce 2, 20094 Corsico, Milano.*

In France: Please write to *Penguin France, Le Carré Wilson, 62 rue Benjamin Baillaud, 31500 Toulouse.*

In Japan: Please write to *Penguin Books Japan Ltd, Kaneko Building, 2-3-25 Koraku, Bunkyo-Ku, Tokyo 112.*

In South Africa: Please write to *Penguin Books South Africa (Pty) Ltd, Private Bag X14, Parkview, 2122 Johannesburg.*